EXCERPTS FROM A HOLY LIFE

Melody Henderson

RoseDog Books

PITTSBURGH, PENNSYLVANIA 15238

The contents of this work including, but not limited to, the accuracy of events, people, and places depicted; opinions expressed; permission to use previously published materials included; and any advice given or actions advocated are solely the responsibility of the author, who assumes all liability for said work and indemnifies the publisher against any claims stemming from publication of the work.

RoseDog Books
585 Alpha Drive, Suite 103
Pittsburgh, PA 15238
Visit our website at *www.rosedogbookstore.com*

ISBN: 978-1-63764-693-9
eISBN: 978-1-63764-733-2

Your words give us life when we were
on the way to destruction

In memory of my older sis Janice,
the first to be born again,
the first to get to go home.

Prologue

"If we claim to be without sin, we deceive ourselves and
the truth is not in us. If we confess our sins, he is faithful
and just and will forgive us our sins and purify us from
all unrighteousness. If we claim we have not sinned, we
make him out to be a liar and his word has no place in
our lives."

1 John 8-10 (NIV)

OH LORD, I DID NOT WANT THIS PAINFUL STORY OF SIN. I did not
want this road that you engineered for this rebellious
daughter. You know Lord, that my flesh, Adam's flesh, has caused
and resisted and lamented along the way the story you orchestrated
especially for me- this worthless-without -you one hundred and
thirty something pounds of flesh. You always knew what it would
take to mold the clay that is me, from before the beginning.

Driven by my pride and innate competitiveness, how I
eventually came to yearn to BE holy. Exactly, Lord! That's right, as
you are always...to bring glory to myself. "Look at me (I fantasized
regarding how HOLY I would make myself)...and I will show you
holiness!" Me me me.

"Get your sorry self out of the way", said You, "and I will reveal
I AM".

"Who is wise and understanding among you? Let them show it by their good life, by deeds done in the humility that comes from wisdom. But if you harbor bitter envy and selfish ambition in your hearts, do not boast about it or deny the truth. Such "wisdom" does not come down from heaven but is earthly, unspiritual, demonic."

James 3:13-16 (NIV)

My Deadly Life of Sin

So how could something I've suggested to be a holy process, my *life*, include in its contents such a vile mess of dead end roads, lustful choices, self sufficiency, prideful independence, an adulterous episode, focus on vanity, continuous self direction, idolatry and complete reliance on my own understanding? How could it include an individual (this writer) who hungrily read, with great earnestness, every single secular current self help book that I was drawn to which taught the current worldly wisdom of my time, filled with man's carnal knowledge, counsel and suggestions? How could a "holy story" of this life of mine, in which I took all that stuff (garbage) and heart fully, intentionally applied it diligently and daily- ever, *ever* qualify for the sacred, indescribably beautiful and elusive adjective of HOLY? Really? Mine a *holy* life? Some will sneer without doubt. Probably many, especially those who know me! I confess that I even patted myself on the back while doing these aforementioned sinful things, because I always thought I was a little special, a bit wiser than most, and maybe, I hoped, doing a better job at seeking worldly knowledge and implementing it, than the next guy or gal.

How could my life be HOLY you ask? This life of pitiful rags worthy of nothing and producing nothing in its independence from Christ but death? Is there any way for the carnal corrupted and helpless life of the flesh to be connected to heaven?

Can you identify with any portion of my personal sin mentioned thus far beloved reader?

You see, dearest, the story the Lord authored for me also has two divorces in it. It has three marriages. It has an abundance of back to back relationships with men during my many years of singleness (which I congratulated myself on, and actually felt prideful during, because I was "monogamous" overall, and waited longer than most of my female peers to commence with intimate sexual relations.) That waiting period was generally three months. (*Did that impress You, my Lord? Or did it break Your heart as you watched, and eventually shatter mine to pieces?*)

I'm a baby boomer. The approved "gold standard" for initiating sexual intimacy in the secular dating world during the 80's and 90's was "on the third date". I haughtily fancied myself as having surpassed that standard, after my first divorce. I sold myself the lie that I was in better standing than my female single counterparts, morality wise, due to my selective abstinence in delaying physical intimacy with any man whom I was in relationship with. Applying my self-thought-out "appropriate waiting period" of about three months, before giving all I had to give physically to a new male partner, led me to ascribe to myself a sense of "higher worth."I fashioned my own carnal sense of moral "purity" by writing my own definition, and shoving aside God's instruction and guidance. Honestly, I had no interest in learning about the teachings of the Biblical God at the time, and as a result I did not pursue any learning. I pridefully constructed and wrote my own moral code.

I thought my own was a moderate plan and a good one, that if adhered to, would never land me in the position of earning the awful adjective of "promiscuous" or viler still, "slut" or "floozy." I fathomed myself to be a "free spirit" who embraced life and all the pleasures it had to offer, a passionate and beautiful woman, whom a man could really love. This is one of the corrupted ideas I used to identify myself as *worthy*. I feared being branded a "cold prude" at least as much as I feared being labeled the opposite extreme. Thus, I rationalized that by diligently following MY own standard, I effectively *lifted myself* to a "higher level" of being in this world. I failed to perceive my sin as sin.

For many years I was quite happy living as the creator of my self conceived higher standard. I did not believe I needed to look any further than my own mind for sound directions. I had designed my own *self* customized righteousness. I bought the lie of the world that "I am enough." Pat on my own back, honor and glory to me, by *me*. I pretty much thought I should have a gold star on my forehead, and my self evaluation was quite favorable. I compared myself most positively to the secular standard of my time to be here. I was little "higher acting" than many of my female peers, most of whom were jumping into bed with men somewhere between the first and third date, to which I thought" tsk tsk". I continued for many years applying the standard I created for myself. How I erroneously leaned on my own understanding!

And now? "SINNER!" screams Satan. "Don't tell those things! Hide yourself in shame and guilt Melody! Why would any true Christian not sneer and scoff at this boring meaningless tale and cast your story aside? IT'S WORTHLESS!"

Has not the blood of Christ been powerful enough to redeem me? Shall I be tied up by the chains of guilt and waste the remainder of my days here? I'm asking God right now what else, if there is any other vileness he would have me confess here that belongs in this piece of the sharing of my story. Something that needs to be mentioned so that some younger woman will perhaps relate to and recognize herself in applying the useless and corrupted natural thinking I describe, and stop in her tracks and examine her life in which she chooses *not* to know and *not* to be directed by the Spirit of our Lord. In which she chooses to *not* to diligently pursue knowledge of and obedience to our Lord through study of his word. Are there more details that I should disclose up front in this tale, at this beginning, to set the accurate perception of the ungodliness of the landscape of my former life in the reader's mind? There is such an abundance of ladders that I placed up against futile dead ended godless walls of fruitlessness that I was extremely eager to climb, and thus I have *much* material to draw from! I climbed many walls leading to being permanently spiritually lost, and to confirming my eternal spiritual death, quite eagerly. My well of past sin is deep. Is yours? I boast not in the level of my sin, truly. There are no spiritually meaningful degrees because *all* of it, without Christ *in* us, will keep us permanently separated from God."There is no difference" Paul writes to the Romans 3:22. I just do not want to fail to honor Him by not mentioning this enormous spiritual truth, and by being transparent and truthful. I am a wretched, depraved sinner. Have been, am, always will be while in this body. Read Romans 7! But I will *not* be condemned to those potentially eternal chains!

"Idiot!" screams Satan. "Do you think this holds any interest for anyone at all? Do you really think that all these trivial sins are a big deal worth anyone taking the time to read about?" If the Lord has engineered this book into your hands, dear reader, please do keep reading.

Let me continue to disclose. Shut up, Satan, I do not belong to you. I failed to bring up my child in the way he should go. How could I when I was so intent on going the wrong way myself while thinking and completely convinced it was the *best* way? It gets worse. I made that choice mindfully and with great intention! And pridefully. It is perhaps going to sound a bit silly to you, but let me try to explain. *Sin ruled me.* Well, that is the three word explanation. I will give you more detail however by sharing with you that around college age I ran, yes *ran* at some point with great disgust and self righteousness and zeal (and much rolling of my eyes) away from the religiosity of my youth. I was raised as, and told by my mom, that we were Catholics. Much of it seemed ridiculous to me, for the most part. It wasn't for me. Why?

I myself had not, in my *own* experience, met any nuns or priests that inspired me or touched my heart in any meaningful or kind way during childhood. (not that many don't exist!) I had never studied the bible with anyone. I was never even taught directly from the bible during childhood, or told that it is our single greatest resource and means by which we can be reconciled to our God. I was never told early on that intimate knowledge of it is essential, as a compass to enable us to live the life God wants for us to have. This life seldom looks like something those immersed in the world with its man made values and carnal pleasures will approve of, promote, admire, champion, desire to emulate or have granted to them. Ironically, it is truly the only *true life*, with life IN it! I recall my mom saying when I was young that one of the priests at our church told her she should not ever try to read the bible on her own, but was to rely on *them*, always, for its interpretation. Is this not what Jewish Rabbi's also do regarding study of sacred scripture? The human Rabbi or human priest is perceived as indispensable to the people.

I recall having to memorize answers to questions in a man constructed catechism, and quaking in my shoes that the nun teaching my class, whose name I never knew, might call on me. I had no relationship with any of them, nor did I observe or do I recall other children having relationships with these teaching nuns. The priests that I was exposed to seemed remote and intimidating, and not one of them ever spoke directly or personally to me as a child. In my mind, it was then and still is now a cold and unpleasant memory tainted with fear and worry. I don't remember experiencing any love there. I think we always remember love.

At sometime in my early twenties I labeled myself "agnostic." I surely didn't need to know God, if there was one, and IF there was, I was certain that fact wasn't actually knowable for certain by mankind. So I purposefully deleted the whole God-program from my existence.

Bad things happen when we attempt to live life as we were not created to live; when we trust in our *own way* and rely upon our *own strength* to carry us through.

I gave birth to a fine son, my only son, my only child, at age twenty six. I *was* actually a virgin up until the time I started dating his father at the age of twenty three. Perhaps I write that from the flesh in a vain attempt to polish up my prior confessed history a bit, and if so, forgive me Lord. I chuckle at myself still sometimes doing this, but I chuckle securely from the safety of the eternal vantage point of *knowing You now.* I liken my own sin to those carnival games where various heads keep popping up from the game board, and the player holds a gavel and is challenged to smash them down one at a time. Every time one gets beaten back under, another pops up from the pit to the surface! Beloved, sin that we polish up, while perhaps seeming less repulsive on the surface from our mere human perception, still leads to spiritual death. We are unable to dress it up or disguise it or even control it on our own, in order that it become acceptable to God. We surely do try though! Friend, pounding those carnival heads of sin down one at a time on your own as they come up regularly, is an exercise in futility! They are not going to ever stop raising up from within you in this present life. When we walk with Jesus we will discover that we sin less over time, but the intense spiritual battle is relentless and hopeless if we battle it by means of our corrupted and useless flesh. I thank God daily it is *He who* through *His mercy and grace has let me taste and partake in* the divine and restful place where the heavy human burden of shame and guilt and deserved just punishment have been demolished.

My parents had raised me to be a "good girl." I was married to my first husband for only a short time, less than a year. I grabbed my infant son in the middle of the night one night in terror, fearing greatly for my life with good cause, and never returned. The next day the strangulation marks appeared on my neck along with other bruising. Confident at this stage of my life that I was completely freed by adulthood from the vice of man driven and man constructed "religion" (the "opiate" of the people!), I vowed that in no way would I be a religious hypocrite when it came to bringing my precious baby Jared up alone.

My own mom had made it clear that she had sent us three girls to Sunday school from a sense of proper "duty" and obligation to "educate", rather than out of an overflow of faith. She gave up church attendance without any obvious or visible moral or spiritual struggle, once her daughters were grown. I deeply believed that I was making a sound, wise and admirable decision in refusing to contaminate my son's life with the example of being a hypocrite, which I would surely be if I taught to his young developing mind what I myself had found no redeeming value in! I ascribed to the concept taught in a contemporary book (published 1960) named "Summerhill" (a radical approach to child rearing) that said a Sunday summer morning spent splashing around in a lake with one's children was more "holy" than the choice to go and sit on hard pews in some church somewhere and listen to a dry sermon and observe religious "rituals." Swimming instead sounded pretty wonderful to me! I bought it hook, line and sinker! Like most of Satan's lies, especially the ones that suck in God's chosen children (even those who have not yet responded to his call), there's some truth in it, enmeshed with subtle, life destroying, life obstructing deceit. Long story short, with the sincerest of self directed mindfulness, I did not teach Jared about anything in the bible (ummm, I did not know much of anything except the ten commandments, and in addition some rote prayers some of which pray to *people* the Lord has used to accomplish his purposes, and not to our God.) This practice of praying to deceased humans offends our God because He was *always from the beginning* the *only One who can change, rescue and deliver*. I did not bring Jared to any church or provide for his spiritual education and training at all. My primary focuses for him were on training in soccer skills, promoting him to be a good student at school, and exposing him to as much of the world as I could. I believed that this sort of foundation would one day lead to his becoming very competent, managing his own life well, and becoming "successful." This success would be measured by world values. As I said, at that time I was deeply convicted that I was acting wisely and with integrity. I abstained for many years from pursuing God, with pride. Sigh. Thank his goodness I eventually responded to God's persistent call, and He knew exactly how to tumble down the walls of stone around my heart and open my closed ears. I repented, and thus have been forgiven. Justified through faith. Jesus's righteousness is what God sees when He looks at me! My friend Marilyn taught me that justified means "just as if I'd never sinned."Does this sound plausible to you, sinner? Can you believe that God is not only well able to convert the ungodly but that He relentlessly pursues them?

My parents were extraordinarily good looking people, and I inherited a fair share of attractive features from each. Although from my viewpoint I was an ugly duckling in early high school, and was almost voted the shyest girl in my 9th grade class because at that time I was so awkward and felt so homely I hardly ever opened my mouth, I eventually blossomed into a pretty teenager later. During my last few high school years, as boys started paying attention to me, my self confidence in my ability to attract men increased. Simultaneously, so did my sense of "self" worth. I would say I became popular. My parents encouraged me and my two sisters that we should date as many boys as possible because this would educate us in the field of "men" and lead to an eventual wiser choice of a husband when the time was right. Their theory sounded good to the ear! "Date around, don't just settle for the first one that likes you."That became their mantra. Education would lead to a more successful life in every area they taught! The dating process was be be viewed as a period of life to immerse ourselves in gathering data on the opposite sex (all while being a "good girl" of course!) and one was to do that by "playing the field." At the same time my folks were actually quite strict with imposing rules, such as every boy had to come into the house and meet them when we got picked up, and we had early curfews. This was my parent's sincere and very well intended idea of providing us with their protection.

My parents seemed to think that if any of their girls ended up marrying the first or second male that we met, that the results would surely be disastrous! They truly believed that they were reducing the odds of any one of us committing to a "cad" by instructing us in this way. I look back now with a firm and clear understanding that they were wrong in this. That belief requires absolutely no faith in our God to be the Director of our paths and the One who makes them straight when we have a personal relationship with Him;

when we delight in Him, and acknowledge Him in *all* of our ways. It requires no faith in Him to direct one's path because they are His eternally starting with salvation, and have been cared for even before one comes to know him as Father. It requires no faith in the wisdom of waiting for His leading, once we do know Him. It does not involve trust in His sovereignty, and faith in His complete overflowing love for His children. It does not involve an understanding of Romans 8:28 or Proverbs 3: 5, 6. It *does* require trusting in one's own ability to "get it right, figure it all out", on their own. I am guilty of doing that for most of my past.

I must add that my wonderful mom and dad were totally devoted to their three daughters' best interests throughout our childhood, and consistently acted according to what *they* understood to be right and true. I shall always love, honor and respect them overwhelmingly for that. Yet we don't always know, do we? We surely don't know truth, and can't know or follow it, when we aren't constantly seeking the truth of God's word by renewing our minds. That means reading and studying and meditating on the contents of the bible, all while asking God to do ongoing works in us that continuously result in keeping our hearts pliable, teachable, and receptive to His transformation; for Him to make our hearts as soft maliable clay, *not stone*. When we do not do these things, whatever the seemingly good rationale or excuse, the result is that we do not know, or forget, what God's love letters and His magnificent story of salvation written over the centuries of human history, tell us. The result of that, if our minds and the eyes of our hearts are never opened to *knowing,* is inevitable eternal spiritual death. That means remaining DEAD in our natural Adamic nature, and we miss out on receiving God's gracious gift of abundant life both *now* while our body lives, and after its demise.

As I pursued my career and further education throughout my twenties and thirties I was oblivious to the fact that I had many painful years and dead end streets ahead of me. I was blind to the fact that I was never going to be able to correct my inherited (from Adam) deadly spiritual life condition by my own efforts and design. I was blind to the fact that I was on a dead end street if I continued on without confident belief in my Redeemer. God patiently allowed me to travel down many paths of suffering and loss and ruin as a result of my own stubborn, determined striving and self confidence in ME. (and in all the secular wisdom in the self help books!) He allowed me to rely on what I am in the natural, ("go ahead then" He said, just as He had indicated to Balaam) on my talents and gifts and attributes that manifested from my DNA, and self formulated beliefs in order that I would exhaust those resources and come to the end of what I can do. It sounds paradoxical to express how grateful I am for that! The Lord brought me through much tribulation in order to teach me what I am apart from Him. The Holy Spirit graciously reminds me continuously to this day, illuminating glimpses of my sinful natural self throughout each day. My Lord brought me through many trials in order to get me in a place of desperation to be saved from what I am, because of the sin that I arrived into the world with upon my first birth.

CHAPTER ONE

✠ This is what the Lord says: "When seventy years are completed for Babylon, I will come to you and fulfill my gracious promise to bring you back to this place. For I know the plans I have for you," declares the Lord, "plans to prosper you and not to harm you, plans to give you hope and a future. Then you will call upon me and come and pray to me, and I will listen to you. You will seek me and find me when you seek me with all your heart. I will be found by you, " declares the Lord, "and will bring you back from captivity." Jeremiah 29:10-14 (NIV)

❂ ❂ ❂

I was in captivity in my own "Babylon" until sometime around the turn of this last century. Let me clarify why I use that particular word, Babylon. The word "Babylon" in a theological sense has become synonymous with a Godless season or seasons in our lives which are ruled by sin and pride. We end up there, dwelling in our collective "Babylons" and remaining as slaves to sin because of our ignorance of, our resistance and our disobedience to, what our Lord teaches us through scripture. We often persist in ignoring or refusing to acknowledge that He has also provided for *all of* us throughout the evidence and records of history, the clear evidence visible in nature, and unique personal experiential evidence given to individuals who are filled with His Holy Spirit. We remain in our ungodliness, often for years, or dreadfully for our whole lives, by ignoring or hardening our hearts to the means by which He draws. In ancient Mesopotamia, mid- millennial B.C., Babylon was a city of wrongful pride and idolatry that temporarily conquered and enslaved God's disobedient chosen people and carried them off into exile. It was God's will that they experience the consequences of their lack of faith and trust in Him. He eventually brought his children out of exile, in His perfect timing, and it was prophesied beforehand so they could recognize *His* hand and see *His* rescue in those exact circumstances. Jerusalem was eventually restored after God's chosen had been in slavery, exiled in Babylon, for 70 years. They were given permission to return if they chose, by a conquering king, in 538 B.C.

We today are also disobedient and rebellious children by spiritual nature, with whom He has made a new covenant that promises us He will restore us to "Jerusalem" and make us ONE with His first chosen but well sifted tribe of Israel, final version, when we repent of our sin, receive and believe the gospel, and surrender our own lives to Jesus.

In November of 2002 I was forty nine years old. I was very fit and conditioned at that time, and had taken up the sport of running for a few years now. I was single, twice divorced (my married years added up between two marriages to a total of "five" over two plus decades), and living alone, as my only son Jared had moved out at age 19. (for rather sad reasons as he had severe ongoing struggles of his own)

Interestingly enough, with the onset of my "fifties" looming ahead of me I had found myself contemplating the onset of aging quite often. Didn't like the thought of it! One of my many false idols back then was my appearance, as it had served me well (from my tainted and erroneous perspective) over the years. I wondered what life would feel like as that "gift" waned. I was reluctant to acknowledge that I would soon have to deal with the humiliations and losses of aging. As with all false idols, we lean on them, instead of God, to infuse life with some immediate sense of meaning and fulfillment, and a sense of belonging and accomplishment. I spent a lot of time thinking about what I might be able to do to sustain a sense of being "able" and "equipped" and "worth something" as I aged. Our culture in general surely does *not* ascribe much or high value to "old people." Surely I could control this somehow! I had discovered through dabbling in running with a neighbor who was willing to coach me, that I had some natural athletic running talent. I reasoned in my mind that surely I would be able to compensate for my own physical aging and general progressive weakening by becoming a great runner! That was going to be my ticket!

At the age of just a month shy of forty six years old, I ran my first Boston Marathon as a "bandit"(i.e. an unqualified runner who jumps the corral fence without a bib number at the start), three and a half months after taking up running. The year was 1999. I completed it in a very respectable time for a "newbie", about four hours and 10 minutes. I felt quite invincible after that athletic accomplishment! What a life high I was on! I was a poster child for the phrase "floating on air"! A patient of mine at work who worked for channel 5 sensed the intensity of my "afterglow"when I chatted with her about it, and the following year asked me to participate in making Channel five's (ABC's) marathon advertisement, which I proudly did.

Running had become my salvation, my God replacement, my false idol.

I qualified to officially run in the Boston Marathon coming up in April of 2000, in October of 1999, at the "Bay State Marathon" with a time of 3:53. That was just by the skin of my teeth. Well, perhaps I should say by the skin of my feet. I had found my "middle age niche" at this point. This would be my focus! No getting old and decrepit for this strong running gal! I'd found a way to give myself immunization from that disgrace of the flesh! I'd discovered my means by which I could redeem myself from the advancing weakness and humiliation of my own aging physical body! As the next few years went by I ran and ran and ran and made many wonderful friends in the running community, which I was drawn to for a multitude of reasons. Not *all* of them were sad from a spiritual perspective. The sheer shining physical health of the sport was one of them. The many friends I made in the running community meant much to me, and I valued them. How I enjoyed my "glory days of running!" I was fully immersed in saving myself, cultivating a whole new identity, and pretty confident that I had found the *way* to do it. After all, some of these local runners were still at it in their seventies and one or two in their eighties. They received attention and respect for their determination, perseverance and athletic ability and seemed to avoid the physical pitfalls that put their peers into nursing care facilities! I lusted for and sought eagerly after that. I was convinced that was where the treasure was.

Simultaneously, as I developed and advanced in my running talent and accomplishments, I continued to seek for a male life partner that would complete what I conceived of as an *almost* perfect, "very together life" according to *world* standards. In my own mind I reasoned that I had my respectable career at a renowned Boston Hospital, had raised an "All American" athlete, a handsome, winsome, and brilliant young man, and that I was a model of good health and fitness. I loved my parents and my family. I was extremely certain I was a "good person." I actually moved in *with* the aforementioned neighbor who had served as my original running coach, into a rented home in Topsfield, MA for about a year, until that relationship dissolved sadly, just like all of my others. He moved out after a big disagreement and I remained in my lovely rented home on Pemberton Road. How tired I became of hearing friends and family say to me "You are just so nice and so pretty we just can't figure out why you've had so much trouble finding a nice husband." I couldn't figure it out either! I was getting quite weary of this unfruitful quest. Was I the problem? I surely doubted that! After all, I *was* nice, educated, hard working, *and* pretty! Why was I reliving this unfruitful cycle of one long term (usually) relationship after another without reaping the desired outcome? I desired and yearned for a loving marriage, one that worked beautifully, like my mom and dad's.

So in February of 2002, now forty nine, once again I got involved in the next relationship in my never ending back to back serial monogamous series. It was with a respected somewhat older runner in the running group, who was fifteen years my senior. He was a really nice fellow, and as a running couple it seemed we were greatly embraced by our mutual running companions, an "extreme" running group called GAC with it's home base in Topsfield. This man and I would run wooded trails with them while training for various running events, literally for hours. Mindlessly and I confess lustfully, I went down that dead end road with a man once again. I was so deceived and lost without even knowing it! I "dated" him for quite a few months and then decided he wasn't going to be "the right one" a short time after he'd asked me to marry him. He was too old for me, I reasoned, and there were a few personality traits that just didn't mesh that well with mine. Same old story. Try, try...nahhh, don't buy. Sigh. It is worthy noting that some months later, after he relentlessly pursued winning me back for quite a while, he met a lovely lady five years younger than I, *twenty* younger than he, and they fell in love and married. My stinking pride was greatly wounded and I felt devastated even though I had not wanted to go down that path with him! I simply apparently was enjoying in an ego satisfying way the flattery and self glory of his yearning and passion for *me*! And retrospectively, I think that probably in my flesh I unconsciously enjoyed the "feminine power" I could wield! External beauty can be a shallow and dangerous earthly power, and potentially obstruct the deeper spiritual life, in a similar way that the material pleasures that wealth can buy can obstruct our perception of whether or not we need to search for God's truth.

I sinfully enjoyed being this older ex boyfriend's temporary idol, and the focus of his heart and desire. It wasn't maliciously calculated, but it was true. It affirmed my good opinion of myself. He had been sending me some really complimentary, flattering love letters. In my competitiveness and sinfully lost state, I even tried to win him away from his new younger girlfriend for a short time, to my shame. I didn't even truly want him for myself! I just wanted to *win*. This is one way that wickedness and darkness reigned in my heart, ruled by my ego. My competitive nature was well honed in many ways besides running.

Now, for a few years preceding this time, starting around the turn of the century, I had begun to take baby steps in seeking God. Remember, this was in my later forties. I had made the decision to re-explore, re-examine, re-visit the question of the identity of Christ. My believing younger sister Diane had invited me and my mom to her church's annual women's retreat for several years in a row. I went with the motivation of getting to spend some quality time with my mom and my sister. God had other plans for me.

Before I had moved to Topsfield, while still living in Salem on Buffum Street, I had decided to read the New Testament, in 1999. I did that because I'd recognized one day that while I'd often had very strong opinions on the Bible and had expressed those vehemently, that I had *never read it*. That's a "DER". That suddenly didn't make much sense to me. Does this describe you perchance? You have a strong opinion regarding the word of God, but without the accompanying intimate familiarity with its contents? During this same time period somehow the book "The Case for Christ" by Lee Strobel came into my hands, and I read it with a genuine need to find absolute truth. I began to wonder if there was a chance that when I'd fled from Catholicism as *I* had experienced it decades ago, if I had "thrown out the baby (Jesus) with the bathwater" (mankind's created useless religious nonsense) Could that be so? Thus I began to actively *seek*.

I tell you this reader because I can look back now and recognize at least *some* of how I was being drawn to faith in Christ. For me, it happened just a little bit at a time, in stages, as far as I am able to discern. God had to bring me through these first few years of reopening the intentionally shut and blind eyes of my heart, 1999 through 2002, making ready the field of my soul, tilling the ground of my heart, before He engineered my very own, custom made for me Damascus Road experience. He used people, circumstances, books, failure, suffering, loss, emptiness, heartbreak, and only He knows what else, to do it.

Using the devastation of my soul (mind, will, conscience and emotions) that was born out of my brokenness stemming from having chased down the same fruitless path with men while searching for the right husband for what seemed like a lifetime, combined with my despair that my beloved son's life seemed to simultaneously be going down the toilet to alcoholism, a situation over which I seemed to have no influence, by mid life in November of 2002 I fell into a severe despondent state of depression (*despite* all the running which had not saved me) and I could not fathom what life was all about.

After this mid-life break up with yet another man, and reading Jon Courson's "A Future and a Hope" that my sister Diane gave me to comfort and encourage, the Lord had finally brought me to a state of readiness and given me ears to hear.

CHAPTER TWO

"I will tell of the kindnesses of the Lord, the deeds for which he is to be praised, according to all the Lord has done for us- yes, the many good things he has done for Israel, according to his compassion and many kindnesses. He said, "Surely they are my people, children who will be true to me; and so he became their Savior. In all their distress he too was distressed, and the angel of his presence saved them."

Isaiah 63:7-9 (NIV)

✠ *I'M AT WORK ONE MORNING* at Brigham and Women's Hospital in Boston, and I am unable to shake the darkness and heaviness in my spirit that is weighing me down. For about 3 years now I have been seeking spiritual truth, yet I am still living very much "in the world" and have, at best, only a very infantile concept of the message of the gospel. I'm forty nine. The year is 2002.

Several years earlier I had responded to an altar call at a non denominational bible teaching Christian church, Calvary Chapel Boston in Rockland, MA. There wasn't much apparent transformation in my behavior or values since. The only reason I had been there in that church that morning was on the invitation of my ex husband Tim, who had been coming up on Sundays from his home on the South Shore to walk my German shepherd Anka for me, since I was injured. My ankle was stress fractured from way too much running! Isn't that interesting? Can you see the irony and the sometimes humorous but always loving hand of God in that? I'd walked up to the front of the church that day in response to Randy Cahill's alter call, *against* my fleshly "better judgment". You see, on that morning as Pastor Randy Cahill had persisted in giving the 4th or 5th altar call, "something" had overridden my own thinking and stubborn resistance, and propelled me to the front of the church. I was on crutches with my running injury, and that seemed like a pretty darn good reason *not* to make my way up to the front of the church to express myself publicly, and look like a fool hobbling down that long aisle. I cared very, very much about what others thought of me and about how I appeared to others. I am so grateful that despite my self, I was not beyond the power of Lord's Almighty hand that day. Is anyone ever? I had just firmly decided that even though it had been a wonderful sermon and I perhaps might walk up to the front if I did not have to hobble up there on crutches, thus I would not, when I was overpowered by a will not of my own. I found myself almost pushing the folks in the pew out of my way so I could profess that I believed Jesus was my Savior and had died for me. I can see in hindsight now that it was He who worked in me "to *will and to act according to his good purpose*". (Phil.2:13 NIV)

Still, at this time, now a few years later, I am living that type of smorgasbord Christianity (take what appeals to you and ignore the rest) and I am extremely immature in Christ. No substantial growth or visible change yet, but a true conversion. I can identify that fact confidently in retrospect, based upon the Lord's ongoing work in me since.

I am feeling so low and depressed on this day, that I can hardly do my work. In my inner being I feel lifeless. I find myself broken up with a man yet once again (the 15 years older than I one), after throwing so much of my heart and soul and body into it. On this particular morning I am supposed to be allergy testing patients, and I am calling them into the procedure room one by one and literally, as my husband Curt would say, "mailing it in." In other words, I am giving it the bare minimum of my effort to get by. I am in such emotional turmoil and total despair, and the life I am living seems to be empty and meaningless and I am drowning in confusion and an aching hollowness. I'm sick and tired of it all. Shattered. I'm at the end of myself, my own strength and my own efforts. Satan seems to be dictating my mood and my lifeless actions, and I have not thought to call upon Jesus's holy name for help. That would be quite unnatural to the carnality I continue to live out of.

Several weeks just prior to this I had attended yet another Calvary Chapel Christian Women's Retreat with my sister Diane and my mom. I still have much of the sweet message on this day in my mind, but can't reconcile it with my circumstances of living. I want to give up, and am rendered impotent to attempt to be anything or to act in any way which requires any kind of genuine mindful presence, effort, caring or energy. I am so *dead* inside. DEAD.

You see, the world will tell you that a "little more license with our sexuality", and ignoring God's command to reserve partaking of this special gift for our marriage partner, is just fine. Secularism actually touts this as a wise idea. "Have some fun single one!" cries the world regarding having casual sex outside of marriage! In fact, don't think of marrying anyone before you thoroughly explore this aspect of who they are! The secular message says to us that *not* remaining within God's revealed and clear boundaries will make for richer living in the right now, and wraps the idea in a package that lures us as tempting choice. Temptation is hard to resist, especially when fueled by natural healthy sexual attraction and hormones.

Secularism says that many of God's directives applied only to ancient and outdated cultures. The absolute truth is that buying into that misguided liberation (not) will brutalize God's female children, and tear their souls to pieces. Without doubt the practice is damaging to men also, but that I can not speak to from personal experience, being female. My own indulgence in what I had determined was *not* going to be sin for *me*, had finally shattered me.

I do feel truly sorry for the patients that get me as their nurse this morning. They are getting the worst of me. I generally feel great empathy for my patients and like to put myself in their shoes and treat them as I would want to be treated if *I* was the one feeling somewhat anxious about the allergy testing procedure which involves lots of pinching and injections. My usual "m-o" would be to distract them away from their fear and nervousness and to get them talking with me if I could, in a sincere effort to take their mind off of what I was doing to their arms, and the pain it was causing. This technique generally worked pretty well with most. I had felt for a long time that I was pretty good at creating relationships, even fleeting brief ones, with my patients.

I am acutely aware that not only am I not making any efforts to be the best "me", or even a watered down version of that, that I am potentially able to be with my morning patients, but that I am not even smiling! How hard is it to *fake* a smile? Sometime mid-morning, I am overcome with dismay by what I know is a sorely lacking and pitiful performance on my part, and I feel shame and remorse. It is bad enough that my own life seems to be coming to absolutely nothing, but now I am wallowing in self pity and dragging down the lives of others by inattention and apathetic treatment towards them! They do not deserve this mismanagement. It occurs to me in *this* moment to pray, since I am convicted that I am helpless to change how I feel, or to get my focus off of my own disappointments and personal sorrows.

I can't recall the exact words but my prayer was something like this, "Lord I can't do this. You see how sad and empty my heart is. You see how little I am caring. I actually do not care anymore. I am disgusted with myself this morning. Help me to rise above what I feel, and to fake it for the sake of not hurting these people and cheating them out of the better service and kindness I could be giving. Come to me and help me to stop ignoring the opportunities to make their visits here more pleasant this morning. *Please help me.*"

I then called the next patient, a young woman, into the procedure room. I literally pasted a very fake and artificial smile onto my face. Drawing my energy to function from a well within that felt completely dry, I brought her into the procedure room and got her seated. Then I started to explain to her nicely, and as if I cared this time, what exactly I was going to be doing, and why. As I recall, she was in her early 30's. I asked her the necessary preliminary medical questions. I did not feel like doing this one bit. It was like swimming upstream. Gloom and lifelessness lurked just behind my phony put on facade. My desire to step my performance up a bit with this patient was born only out of some wee bit of compassion that was still existent within me, along with some languishing ability to empathize....both virtues seemingly and rapidly dying a final death. Flesh wise I wanted desperately to focus only on poor me, savor my depression and self pity, and roll around in despair. I wanted to ditch what I was now doing, and escape into a permanent sleep. Yet I do also confess that I recall that in my heart that I did simultaneously yearn to be pleasing to the Lord, even though I was attempting to accomplish that out of my own strength by manipulating my own behavior. (instead of *dying* to what I am in the natural, and letting my hidden life in Christ rule/live in me) (Gal.2:20; Romans 6:6; Col. 3:3)

So as I said, I am now engaged in light conversation with my female patient, and forcing myself to go through "the motions". It was so much effort and weightiness to do so....to propel myself to keep going with this phony act. Like walking through thick cement. I was kicking against the goads of my flesh...struggling and fighting to do the right thing; against forces, (evil powers and principalities) which I have zero power to conquer.

I was sitting at a procedure table across from the young woman, but then noted I required another testing extract, and I rose from my seat to walk over to the fridge about four feet away, where the allergenic extracts were kept. I had already determined that the patient was married, and decided in an effort to continue the conversation, not that I cared too much, to ask her if she had any children.

"Oh yes I do" she answered. "I just had a baby a month ago." "Oh isn't that wonderful" I lied, (really *didn't care*)... "and did you have a boy or a girl?"

"I had a little girl."

ASK HER WHAT SHE NAMED HER BABY BECAUSE THAT IS MY MESSAGE TO YOU.

There appeared a dominating thought in my mind that was not of me! It spoke without words, but with great clarity, and I was taken by extreme surprise. For a moment I briefly judged myself as having gone insane. Oh great, I sourly thought, now I am not only pitifully despondent but I also suffer with the psychological diagnosis of "magical thinking." I could *not* comprehend what was going on!

I TOLD YOU TO ASK HER WHAT SHE NAMED HER BABY. IT IS A MESSAGE FROM ME TO YOU.

I gave up the effort to figure this out and surrendered to the intrusive directive that had taken dominion over my mind. I shall never ever forget the memory of where I was standing in that room, or the angle of my body, as I turned with unmindful obedience to the uninvited voice in my head and said to the young mother "And so what *did* you name your baby?"

She looked up at me and replied, "HOPE."

Oh Lord, I am ON MY KNEES thanking you even all these years later for your great intrusion into my life, which was truly only a deadly walk only towards death as I was drowning in my sin and separation from you. It was not any true life at all. I was a dead woman walking. In Jesus's name I thank you!

❂ ❂ ❂

I remember in the afterglow of our Lord speaking directly to me while I was in this low valley of my earthly walk, how every negative feeling that I had been smothering to death in, was decimated. I was on an incredible spiritual high that I could not even put words to and I wanted to dance through the rest of my day! In my heart, I did dance. The one and only God of the universe had clearly spoken to *me. To this day any time I find myself in a desert season of my life I think back upon that magnificent moment of my eternal life, and meditate with wonder on what our Lord did for me.*

"You are the God who sees me,"for she said, "I have now seen the One who sees me."

Genesis 16:13 (NIV)

"Then Jesus told them a parable to show them they should always pray and not lose heart."

Luke 18:1(NET)

CHAPTER THREE

"Surely God is my salvation, I will trust and not be afraid.
The Lord, the Lord, is my strength and my song; he has
become my salvation."

Isaiah 12:2 (NIV)

"Salvation comes from the Lord."

Jonah 2:9 (NIV)

"There are six things the Lord hates, seven that are
detestable to him, haughty eyes..."

Proverbs 6:16, 17 (NIV)

✟ IT IS THE YEAR 2006 NOW, and I am alone in church one late
September Sunday morning at Calvary Chapel Boston, located
in Rockland, MA, where I first publicly testified to my new faith. I
live alone in an apartment in Salem at this time, and the Lord has
been growing my faith through the years and teaching me that
which He would deem for me to know. I don't mind traveling to the
South Shore to attend services even though I am on the North Shore,
because I know there is a God fearing Spirit directed steadfast
humble senior pastor there named Randy Cahill and I am (the Lord
has) drawn (me) to his teaching. It was he that baptized me at his
church's women's retreat in a pool a few years back, and I love to

get fed by listening to the Lord's messages delivered through him. I sit alone as I always do, and I don't mind at all. I do not feel alone.

On this particular morning, I am grieving. My wonderful, honorable, devoted Italian earthly father had passed away just a few short weeks beforehand, in mid September. I was just crazy about my World War 11 hero dad. He was a sweet, humble, handsome and noble man, who loved to help others. He was a peacemaker in our family and in his workplace, and usually the one that family members would seek out for council and direction, as needed, on multiple life issues. He was cherished and respected and trusted implicitly, within our extended family. Always calm in a storm, he ironically was the parent who always told us girls to pray throughout our childhood, although he never went to church. Perhaps he himself learned to pray during those days in the 1940's while landing with the 248th Combat Engineers infantry division on Utah Beach on D-Day, as a very young man, and subsequently sweeping through Europe's enemy occupied territory to prepare the way for Patton's tanks, which followed. You know what they say about there being no atheists in foxholes! Perhaps that is true, I never asked my dad *why* he always told us to pray. I wish I had.

I generally arrive there early at church, and as I am waiting for the worship and service to get going I begin to look around at the people already seated. My eyes land on Lindsey Lyons (her future and current married name), who is Pastor Randy and his wife Cheryl's daughter. She is a teenager at this time, and I have often admired and thoroughly enjoyed listening to her sweet lovely voice when she leads worship. A critical spirit within me immediately jumps to life!

My thoughts go something like this "Wow, she is *really* not dressed appropriately as the pastor's daughter. Way too casual! She needs to take that baseball cap off. And are those ripped jeans?

Geeeez...she's chewing gum in church. Someone needs to speak to that girl and help her get it right."

The service starts. My focus comes off of criticizing and tearing apart sweet Lindsey within my mind, and shifts to the front of the church. I find myself occasionally softly weeping and wiping away tears as Randy's message (that is, the Lord's Spirit speaking through him) is instrumental in softening my heart and paving the way for Jesus to rule in me. My grief over the loss of my dad bubbles up and I am unable to contain it. So I quietly weep. I am sure my aching heart was written on my face. I feel extremely vulnerable! I want to both conceal my grief and not look foolish, and simultaneously to be understood and to receive comfort. What vessels of contradictory feelings we all are!

The service ends and with blurry wet eyes I rise up out of my pew and turn to my right to enter the aisle to leave.

I almost jump as unexpectedly there is *someone* standing *right there* in my path, blocking my way. *IT IS LINDSEY.* I do not recall her exact words, but the essence of what she says to me in that moment is "I looked over at you and saw that you looked upset this morning. Is there anything that I can pray for- for you?" I am extremely, yes immensely humbled in this moment as I realize that the ONE my own eyes picked out of the full congregation, hundreds of attendees, to tear down in my mind this day, has chosen *me*, out of *all those people*, as her ONE, to help. Lindsay by the way does not even know me, or have a personal one on one relationship with me. To her at this time I am simply a distressed, much older stranger attending and worshiping at her church.

Lindsey's tender hearted kindness, a clear fruit of the spirit radiating from her, triggers me to blurt out my own heart and my circumstances to her. "Oh Lindsey I am crying because I just buried my father a few weeks ago and I'm so sad. I'm Diane Danahy's sister

Melody, I don't know if you remember me from any of the retreats. It is so kind of you to come over." Lindsey took my hand and sweetly prayed with me for comfort and for the Lord's arms to be around me. I felt her *love* and *caring*. I could hardly breathe as I left the church.

You see, I saw that once again that our Lord, my Father and yours, loved me enough on that day to remarkably and simultaneously do multiple things for me all at once. In the gentlest of ways, I was disciplined *and* taught *and* deeply comforted. The Father, our Father, sat back while my sinful nature ruled and listed every thing in my judgmental mind that was wrong and improper ,from my haughty sinful view, with Lindsey's teenage dressing choices. Then, through His Holy Spirit He directed her, who was one *willing* and *able* to hear and heed His directive, able to let Him work *through her*, to come over to a much older woman and risk putting herself on the line, for my sake. I don't believe she ever hesitated to traverse that church at the Lord's direction, to make her way to the saddened woman. The fact that she actually did so took my breath away.

As I drove out of the parking lot and away from Calvary Chapel Boston in Rockland that day, I was overwhelmed by the incredible mercy and everlasting kindness of the Lord. I realized that it had been His plan all along to use the hands and feet and voice and *heart* of Lindsey, His own daughter that I had judged mercilessly, to minister to me in my grief and loneliness. What an extraordinary and radical and lasting lesson for me.

Lindsey, I have never shared that story with you or written it down until now, twelve years later as I write this, but how grateful I am as your sister in Christ that you acted on that day. You got it right. I'll bet you don't even remember, but I always will. The Lord of the whole universe had actually ministered to me, using you, and despite the lump in my throat as I thought the events over, I understood at a new level what our Lord means with his command to us "DO NOT JUDGE." He is the only actual teacher who can accomplish anything in us and with us, Who can actually *change* us and make us into what we are not by the power of His Holy Spirit, and He often works through us to accomplish *His* will, as you well know.

So friends, let's ask for the help of the Spirit to enable us to hear and heed His command, and always remind one another *"do not judge."* He hath opened the eyes of this judgmental woman! He is able to take what I *am not* and maketh me as though I *am.* (Romans 4:17) He does this in an ongoing way as I ask for the help of the Spirit to "die to" what I am in my inherited Adamic *self without Christ.* I confess that I often stumble and backslide, and I require constant correction and God's discipline, redirection, intervention and mercy. From haughty sinful judge of others (that which I surely *am in the natural) transformed* into humbled, repentant, willing-to-learn and be made *into* a new creation daughter! He makes me into what I am *not and can not be on my own,* since I'd rather follow my own will while living from my flesh. *He* makes me willing to see there is a better way and it is *He* who sets me anew on his loving path that leads me into LIFE!

The *only* life.

"Why do you look at the speck of sawdust in your brother's eye and pay no attention to the plank in your own eye?"

Matthew 7:3 (NIV)

"for it is God who works in you to will and to act in order to fulfill His good purpose."

Phil. 2:13 (NIV)

CHAPTER FOUR

"He bestows on them a crown of beauty instead of ashes,
the oil of joy instead of mourning, and a garment of
praise instead of a spirit of despair."

Isaiah 61:3 (NIV)

✠ IT IS OCTOBER 26ᵀᴴ, 2010. It is very, very early in the morning,
and I am in a state of extreme despair and mourning. This is
four years after my Dad's death now. I am up very early at four
thirty a.m. and preparing for my long commute into work as a nurse
in Boston, while weeping and gulping back sobs. I had been
informed late in the evening just the night before that my son's
girlfriend Kim that he lived with in New York City, had started labor
pains. I had been told about the pregnancy so this was no surprise,
and I knew that I was about to imminently become the grandmother
of a baby granddaughter. I could not find it in me to rejoice and was
devastated that I was actually *grieving* this now occurring birth.
How counter intuitive and *wrong* this grief felt! I knew that my
sorrow came from a heartsick, wounded place within...it seemed so
horribly awful to be *grieving* at a time when it was my right to be
rejoicing, was it not? Does not a woman have a right to rejoice in the
birth of a grandchild-her *first* biological granddaughter? Why was
this joy denied to me? It seemed like just another take-away on my
lengthy list of loss. I felt numb with shock and a depth of sadness I
had never yet known.

You see, my son had already sired one precious little boy into this world. Tyler was five years old at this time, and living with his mother in Revere, MA. The relationship between my son and Tyler's mom had blasted apart early in Tyler's life as a result of my son Jared's progressive alcoholism. It had been heart wrenching to witness Tyler's suffering as an innocent young victim of this disastrous relationship. From his earliest years, Tyler harbored memories of attachment to a father figure that he called "dad", so when Jared disappeared from his life *totally*, when he was around three, it was impossible to shelter Tyler from feeling the deep loss, and from being hurt. What could one say? It is well beyond our young children's understanding when they are abandoned. They can not realize it has nothing to do with *them*. When I took Tyler sometimes for a weekend he would desperately say to me "Mimi where is that man that I used to call dad that went away to New York?" His pain, loss and unfulfilled longing shattered my heart. His need for a father, his own father, was palpable. It haunted me. It sickened my heart which already was often numb with my own pain over my son's alcoholism. It was just yet another layer of harm rendered onto another human being by the weapons and vileness of Satan, in this case the curse, the power of the DNA within my own son consuming him alive with it's inherited propensity for alcohol. Perhaps if I had had Godly wisdom in my past life and had known the Lord....I teetered on the dangerous precipice of taking personal responsibility for every single person's mistakes, painful paths and heartaches, instead of submitting to the truth that our deadly sin natures were and are the root problem; the absence of righteousness in us all. (Romans 3:23) Disregarding the teachings of God and disobedience always leads inevitably to pain and disaster.

I could not imagine that anything about this was going to turn out well. How I desired, relished, reveled in the idea of welcoming a little granddaughter into this world, under more stable and Godly circumstances in the parents' lives. But after being intimately connected to, and a witness to little Tyler's heartache and loss and suffering that stemmed from *not* having a present and participating father equipped and able to love and guide him at such a tender vulnerable age, it wrenched my heart in two to think of the sorrows these terribly unwise choices on the part of new mother Kim and my son Jared would render upon all...including themselves and myself. Yet it was the thought *especially of* the future harm to the child now in the process of coming into this world to begin that portion of her life lived outside of the womb, that slayed me. The mother and the father quite clearly to me had their ladders leaning against the crumbling walls of worldly advice and secular values and self fulfillment. (sound familiar?) Sinking sand. I knew all too well about what is reaped from unbiblical choices sown, from my own life, and also from watching the life of Tyler and his mom, whom I loved. She had lived with me for about a year after she became pregnant at 19. I saw much of myself at that age mirrored in her.

So I wept almost uncontrollably on the way to work that morning. This sorrow felt like more than I could handle. I could not bear it. I couldn't believe that this was all happening....*again. I was praying for Jared constantly,* but as of yet I had not seen the Lord's hand move in his life. Had not the Lord *told me* to HOPE? What hope was there in this new dire set of circumstances? What was going to be sown from *this? Two unmarried parents and a father, having failed the first child, still in bondage to alcohol.* And to make things seem even more vile and bitter- the truth was that I would have welcomed either mother of my grandchildren, both beautiful, bright young women...into my heart as their mother-in-law. Yet it was not to be.

Today was my mother's birthday also. This day that *she* was about to become a great grandma for the second time through my son, but this time to a little girl, was *her* birthday. There are no coincidences in God's kingdom. So what did that mean?

I arrived at my place of work very early and drove into the parking lot off of Route 9 and parked my car in front of the building where I worked. Brigham and Woman's Hospital had most of their ambulatory practices located there. I sat in the car trying to collect myself for awhile, before I opened the car door to get out. I was screaming out to Jesus in my inner being, but had nothing but tears and a broken heart to offer Him.

It was about six thirty in the morning. The parking lot is typically quite deserted at that time. Most patient appointments aren't scheduled until eight or nine a. m. As a result, I am very startled as through the blur of my tears I see a stranger, a lone woman a little older than I, walking directly and purposefully towards me!

I stop in my tracks, somewhat stunned as this has never occurred before...and on *this* of all days when I am so poorly equipped to deal with another person! Is she going to rob me? She doesn't appear threatening! It is quite early and still somewhat dark in the parking lot.

She approaches me with gentleness, and somewhat apologetically. "I am sorry to intrude on you" she says, "but I have been sitting in my car over there watching you cry, and I can see you are greatly distressed about something. The Lord said to me "Go over there and talk to that woman." I can not believe what I am hearing! If ever the Lord has sent an angel in earthly form to me, then surely it is her.

As I try to shake off my disbelief that this is even happening, the flood gates of my mouth open and I begin to pour out the tale of the current events of the circumstances of my life, and the sorrowful woeful story of my son and his babies' lives to her, while still crying.

She puts her arms around me and holds me. The she says to me "I understand some of your pain, I was raised by two alcoholic parents." She goes on speaking softly giving me encouraging words, and assuring me that everything is going to be alright. I am pretty sure she prayed with me but in all honesty I was so intensely emotional that I don't remember that part.

What I do remember very clearly is those moments of love in action unfolding between me and that dear stranger, an unknown sister of mine, whose name I never asked. As I was held and comforted by her, I was held and comforted by Jesus himself. I am certain of this. I recall how *thoroughly and completely and deeply comforted I was.* How crazy and impossible it seemed from the capacity of my human mind to comprehend that the Lord had engineered her into that parking lot early that very morning, right near my car with a good view of me, in His perfect timing, to minister to me, his broken daughter. Yet I *knew* that that was exactly what the Lord had done for me. He is indeed near to the brokenhearted.

You see, not ONLY was there the wonder resounding within me as to the amazing divine timings of this whole episode as I parked in the parking lot that morning. There was also the incredulous recognition of what a marvelous, compassionate, richly faithful daughter of the Lord that woman, that Jesus filled loving stranger had become, *despite* the circumstances of her birth and the addictive illness's of her two parent's! What an immeasurable encouragement to me! Our God was bigger and more powerful than all of that human weakness and propensity towards sin! His ways trump, supersede, override, conquer, banish and transcend the harm Satan renders in our lives when we believe in and trust *Him*. He makes all things possible and he takes the evil that touches his children's lives and makes it work *for their good.* Surely if you believe you know the verse? (Romans 8:28)

I was miraculously encouraged and rejoiced on this day of my greatest sorrow. My mom *and* my grand daughter's birthday... somehow, the Lord whispered His presence to me through that. I would always be reminded of this child on this special day. Whether or not I ever got to assume the cherished role of grandmother to her in this life was up to the Lord. Whether or not my son rose out of his own bondage by the power of God and became her acting earthly father, was up to the Lord. If he said no, it was not to be, he would *still* be my peace and joy, he would be my Deliverer, as always HE IS.

❖ ❖ ❖

"The Lord is close to the brokenhearted and saves those who are crushed in spirit."

Psalm 34:18 (NIV)

"If we are thrown into the blazing fire, the Lord we serve is able to rescue us from it, and he will rescue us from your hand, O king. But even if he does not, we want you to know, O king, that we will not serve your gods or worship the image of gold you have set up."

Daniel 3:17-18 (ESV)

"Praise be to the God and Father of our Lord Jesus Christ, the Father of compassion and the God of all comfort, who comforts us in all our troubles, so that we can comfort those in any trouble with the comfort we ourselves have received from God."

2 Corinthians 1:3-4 (NIV)

"Now hope does not disappoint, because the love of God has been poured out in our hearts through the Holy Spirit whom he has given us."

Romans 5:5 (NIV)

CHAPTER FIVE

"I cried out to God for help; I cried out to God to hear me. When I was in distress, I sought the Lord; at night I stretched out untiring hands and my soul refused to be comforted."

Psalm 77:1-2 (NIV)

"For it has been *granted* to you on behalf of Christ not only to believe on him, but also to suffer for him, since you are going through the same struggle you saw I had, and now hear that I still have."

Philippians 1:29
(NIV; emphasis by author)

✠ SO MANY OF THESE CHAPTERS OF MY PATH made holy by the Lord tell of personal tears, heartbreak, failures, angst, loss, and suffering. I believe they all do, actually. I make a point of emphasizing this truth because these very kinds of painful things in our lives work to establish the fertile soil, the *ground* in which the Lord brings us to the cross and then *grows* us in knowledge of Him, trust in Him, faith in who He is, and ability to persevere through every situation via His strength, not ours. These are our victories in Christ, which are a result of His work in us, and the means by which *we become His eternal trophies*. This repetitive process is the road that leads to the formation of Godly character, and to our *hope* being placed *only* in who He is! (Romans 5:3-4)

God makes us into what we can not be.

We are perpetually given the comforting assurance that He loves us! I thank the Lord that my hope is not rooted in who and what I am, but anchored firmly to Him. I thank Him that He employs every difficulty in my life as a tool of his grace to produce Godly character in me. I echo James in crying out to my brothers and sisters to "count it all as joy!" I urge you to trust him with *all* of your heart, with everything in your life. EVERYTHING! He is sovereign over *all*. Do we know what all means? It means *all*.

This particular year of my life is 2005. At this time I am living in a condominium in Salem, MA that I have purchased along with my son Jared. He was very brilliant at business, and was making a very good income at the time, working at a mortgage company. Against my better judgment, I had bought this property with him. I had formerly resisted, for many months, his request to purchase property together. His credit score was not good, although he could afford a mortgage, so he'd asked me to partner with him. As his parent, this did not seem to me like a "healthy path." I suspect many parents who have co-signed with adult children or supported them in business ventures might agree. When the nineteen year old mother of my grandson, Bridget, became pregnant, my better judgment flew out the window. My distorted need to rescue everyone was triggered. All I could think about was the welfare of the unborn baby. I bought the condo with Jared using my own good credit, and Bridget lived there with us.

Bridget is painfully young and immature by virtue of her age at the time to be in this position, yet in a practical sense, she's an able and eager mother. Jared is excrutiatingly sick with the disease of advancing alcoholism which Bridget had not yet fully realized, nor had I. I had not become certain of the ugly fact until this very year while living with him again. The last Jared and I had shared a family household was six years ago, when he was nineteen years old. At that time the alcoholism was just getting revved up, and it hadn't been clear to me during the ensuing years whether he actually had the progressively destructive disease, or was simply a young man sowing way more than his share of "wild oats."

All hope that the past years had been just a "wild rebellious season" of his development was quenched, as I viewed the ongoing ripening of his flesh and soul sickness at close range, while living in this condo with him and Bridget. I recall the actual moment that I knew for certain he had inherited his biological father's disease, and yes, my own maternal grandfather's disease. One night, a cluster of his male friends carried him inside in the wee hours of the morning. He was semi conscious and his eyes seemed to be rolling back into his head. One of those "friends" said to me "Your son Jared drinks like he used to play soccer." That was terrifying! Jared had been an All American soccer player at St. John's Prep and taken every soccer award available in New England in 1998, his senior year. Seven of them. MVP, All New England, All Catholic Conference and blah blah blah. All worthless in eternity. My heart sank. There was no more denying it.

He would take off on two or three day "benders" during this time, during this living arrangement, abandoning Bridget and infant Tyler for the weakness and desire of his flesh, alcohol. The temptation of the alcohol seemed to win. Every. Single. Time. The place where he would go to drink endlessly was most often the wicked and decadent godless home of two much older men, Peyton and Paxton. They lived only a few miles away from the condo where we lived. They seemed to be Satan's chosen agents to lure Jared back into the drink and drunkenness every time he had one or two weeks or even a few days of sobriety under his belt. Also, he hung out with a few other men of disreputable character, one who would visit Jared at our home and almost always bring along a bottle of vodka. He would compete with Bridget for Jared's attention and loyalty. "Bad company corrupts good character." (1st Cor.15:33, NIV) Not that others were to be blamed for what Jared was drowning in. It was inherited *sin*. Period. The same for his friends.

We all drown in our sin, that's the way it is without faith in Christ. The weakness of the flesh in a multitude of forms can be passed along genetically. Sin is surely passed along spiritually. We may all make the argument that it is "not our fault" that we arrive freshly out of the womb this way, with these sinful propensities and natural predispositions, yet that is not where God asks us to be accountable. The Bible makes it clear that our flesh is embedded with a sinful nature. It is what we do with that knowledge once God brings us to it, and what choices we make *after* God makes it clear to us how unable we are on our own to fix our inherent sin condition, that leaves us in our condition of spiritual death or gives us life in Jesus. The "prettier" sins separate us just as effectively from our holy God as the varieties that tend to disgust and revile us. Yet in our ignorance of Godly knowledge we often erroneously feel *comparatively* self righteous when examining the sins of *others*. We all sometimes attempt to ease our consciences by pointing to those whom we evaluate to be more unrighteous than we are. This is done from the perspective of flesh looking horizontally at flesh. From God's perspective, any *self* righteousness derived from a comparative scale of humanly defined righteousness, is no righteousness at all.

Sin's original entry into our world occurred at the point of mankind's choice to digress from God's loving direction. The Bible tells us that Adam was the first to break God's original command, together with Eve, and that we were "in Adam"- thus bearers of his fallen nature; yet we also were (are) "in Christ", and may bear *His righteousness* if we believe. (1 Corinthians 15:21-22) After receiving the *written* law from God via Moses at Mount Sinai, God's chosen people continued to prove throughout history that they (we) could not adequately keep it on their/our own. In other words, we can't keep it sufficiently enough to fix what we *are*, because of sin living in us. We are unable to save ourselves by rectifying our own sin condition, try as we might. After Adam, we were no longer protected from sin or it's consequences because even though we can't truly absorb or understand it *now*, we were *truly* all "in Adam" when he sinned, just as all believers are *in Christ* now, and have been crucified with Him. (Galatians 2:20)

We are all sheltered and blessed by adhering to God's directions which are always for our ultimate spiritual good. (Genesis 3:3-6) He loves us far beyond that which we can conceive of. Do not feel dismayed, dear one, that the minds we have been given are drastically limited in their ability to understand the ways and orchestrations of God. If we could comprehend and explain all of it, we would be equal with Him and would not need to seek Him or depend on Him. Faith would not be necessary. In Deuteronomy 29:29 it is written:

"The secret things belong to the Lord our God, but the things revealed belong to us and to our children forever, that we may know all the words of this law."

(NIV)

The very same law that our Savior fulfilled perfectly in our behalf, ushering in the age of grace.

Back to my story. The vileness, foulness and separation from the Lord's will evident in my son's friends' lives rendered its destructive effects. Technically, from the perspective of the spiritual realm, I believe they were actually, at least in one way, no worse inwardly. They were no more corrupt in their inner being than we all are, as far as all of us having been born with that *same* sinful nature. It can be hard to perceive humanity's collective sin this way, but it is true. The difference between God's chosen saved and the forever lost is that for reasons far beyond my ability to discuss, but will attempt to express in a few words, is that some humans choose to never seriously seek God or acknowledge evidence that He *is*. God's word tells us that they are without excuse, because there is so much evidence that testifies to His *being*. Some choose to resist every evidence of His reality and His glory. Unfortunately, they persevere in this stance instead of allowing the Lord to bring them to faith in which *He* then will be the very means by which they will be equipped to persevere. They fail to knock boldly, or even hesitantly, on the door of heaven looking for answers. Our Father *is there*, so much closer and present than we can ever realize in the now, waiting with open loving arms to embrace his repentant children and bestow complete forgiveness. He is yearning to bestow on them the treasure and power of His Holy Spirit, to accomplish the purposes He has for their lives.

The two men whose home Jared regularly hung out at to wildly drink and party were surely used by the evil one to help destroy. They were locusts. Peyton and Paxton had parties and orgies at their home that were nothing less than satanic. Bridget, Tyler's mom, would be devastated every time she realized that he was off binge drinking again, and I have no doubt that the abundance of alcohol was the strongest draw for Jared. I would come home from work and find Bridget just *beside* herself, full of despair, inconsolable. It seemed to me that these two evil men were competing with Bridget for Jared's time and loyalties driven by their disdain towards the beautiful young woman he loved. I theorized that their obvious deep hatred of women was expressed in their continuous verbal degrading of her. They were always invalidating of her worth, at every opportunity, to Jared. Anyone who has ever lived with a person in bondage to alcohol *knows* that they *always* choose to go with the one who is waving the bottle in the air, the one inviting them to come and drink with them. That is the way it goes, unless our God intervenes. He is mighty to save and *will* do so if He chooses, in *His* timing! That most often looks radically different than the way *we* would have written the script. Yet it is our God who is the author of our salvation, not us.

On *this* particular day Jared has taken off yet once again. The pain of it seems unbearable. My life has become completely unmanageable while living in this household with Jared, young Bridget, and precious baby Tyler. The Lord has sent me this year to learn about some practical, healthy Godly principles of dealing with a loved one's alcoholism. He has ushered me to Al Anon. I am an infant in "the program", yet I am recognizing in my learning curve that the principles and sayings they teach are in alignment with God's word, in which I am also simultaneously being grown in Godly knowledge, wisdom, and understanding. This recognition assures me that I am where the Lord wants me for my good *at this time*. "Apart from me you can do *nothing*" says Jesus. "We admit we are powerless over alcohol" (i.e. our sin nature) "but that God is not and we must make a decision to turn over our wills and our lives to His care" teaches this program. It is full of widely diverse groups of people, some who know the one true God, and many others who do not. Most have had so much emotional pain, and are in what seem to be disastrous relationships. They are sick and tired and worn out, often hopeless, filled with a desperate sense of futility in what *they* are not able to do, that is, make their beloved family member sober up. Free them from their bondage. The attendees are ripe for change, and ripe for the restoration that only Jesus can bring.

A well run Al Anon program facilitates compassionate support and love between the members. It encourages despairing family members, as it steadfastly highlights the message for them to turn their loved one completely over into the care of God. (however they conceive of Him in their present moment) Do you think that's okay? I believe it is, because our God meets His children where they are at, and is well able to correct drastic spiritual misconceptions over time, as He teaches His own to walk in His power. Children of God are brought to the discovery, usually with much kicking and screaming, that they have *no power without God with them.*

A major premise of Al Anon is to stop trying to fix and help your beloved alcoholic yourself. Why? You can't. STOP IT. YOU are unable to fix their deepening and entrenched sin, loved one. Detach! Guard your heart! Get on your knees and focus on your faith in Jesus and trust Him to hear your prayer and accomplish what *your* own flesh can not do. The battle you wage in order that *you* may *be* your child's (parent's, spouse's, sibling's) savior will destroy you, become a false idol that consumes and distracts you. It will be a path to further harm, and alienate them further from you. Your only hope that can offer authentic hope is for you to *run* into the arms of our Almighty God, Who is not only in control, *He* is the source of all healing and transformation. We need to find our comfort, strength, security and serenity via faith in His power only, *not* our own.

Detaching from one you dearly love is completely impossible without a deep knowledge of and trust in God, which means believing in and relying completely on His divine power, an ability which is only birthed and sustained through faith. And faith is born from God creating in us ears to hear, and eyes willing to spiritually *see* as He himself opens the "eyes of our hearts." It is grown out of our divinely engineered experiences, which we may count on His provision for.

We are told directly by Jesus to *share* our burdens with one another and also to *cast* them onto the Lord. "Carry each other's burdens, and in this way you will fulfill the law of Christ." (Gal. 6:2 NIV) Christians are required to compassionately assist those who are being crushed by life's unbearable sorrows and troubles. We must trust that God will bring these people *to us*. I believe God gives this directive through Paul because He knows how fragile we are, and that it is not good for us to isolate ourselves with the kind of heart and soul pain that addictive life issues cause. That isolation from others leads to our becoming very sick and depressed. In that state we are impotent and quickly become an unusable instrument.

We are spiritually wired to commune and fellowship! I once had a wonderful, Godly, but not infallible pastor who advised his flock to not ever attend secular help groups such as the ones available to the public like AA and Al Anon. He criticized the value of them constantly. While the Lord surely does *not* choose to direct *all* of His children to these secular groups, and definitely does not *need* or *require* them to accomplish His purposes, I do know that He directs *some* of His children to them, because I was one of them! Don't be afraid to go. The Lord will let you know if it's not where He wants you.

It is the Lord who got me there, into this community of heartbroken, shattered people, and I *was helped*. The Lord eventually used me in those groups full of suffering people to speak to whomever He had there on any given day about my faith, and how my faith intersected with my pain, but not before He had me humbly accept the "coaching" and learn how to courageously apply Al Anon's Godly practical principles to my relationship with my son. I would have *never been able to benefit* if I did not know the Lord! I believe in that statement lies the bridge between what this pastor suggested to his flock to avoid, and what I knew to be true. God is omnipresent. Thus He works *everywhere*. I must say that just as it is true that there are some church attendees who are propelled to go to church for all the wrong motives and end up worshiping all the wrong things, it is also true that there are a percentage of Al Anon attendees that end up worshiping the "program" itself and they make the mistake of wanting to give the "program" credit, *instead of our one powerful God who can work powerfully within it's setting.*

It is good for people at end of their rope to share their needs for healing, hope and encouragement. It is good to share your heart aches and disappointments. It is good to let down the facade of pretending you are enjoying a life that is working just great all the time. God comes near.

Our God truly does work anywhere He wants to! He is not restricted! While it's true some believers are put off by folks in Al Anon who verbally shower glory on the "program" as if it is something sacred in itself, failing to give God the credit as *the One* way to *all healing*-this is no greater or lesser sin than we will find in the church itself. The believer who is led to Al Anon must be certain to *attribute any good that comes of attendance and application, to our God.* We must learn to say about everything "it is the Lord!" Ours is the responsibility to point others to Him. Believers partaking must be diligent to gently let the others know, as God supplies the opportunity, that it is not the "program" that saves them from heart destruction and hopeless despair. We do not want ourselves or others to fail to recognize our *only* hope- our God, our Jesus, present and available to us everywhere. I can testify that God uses people participating in this program as vessels that His Holy Spirit *will* speak through, to those writhing in the agonies and tragedies of alcoholism. It has been my experience that He often does! *May it be true* that occasionally in the past and according to God's purpose and pleasure in acting through me, an earthen vessel with a treasure within, seeds for the kingdom were planted. All glory be to God.

So one thing I am saying dear reader who may have trials similar to mine, is that Al Anon has the potential be a form of missionary work also. These rooms filled with hurting people desperate for help are fields *rich* for sowing seeds of the love of Jesus. Do not forget, believer, that where you go goes the Spirit within. If you are a believer who feels inclined to try a secular program then do not fear stepping out in faith to see what or whom the Lord may have waiting for you there. Commune continuously with *Him*. He will show you assigned work which differs little (from a spiritual perspective not at all) from that of a missionary heading into the jungle with prayers of bringing the gospel to a pagan, primitive tribe. Even in your grief, yours can be the joy of spreading the gospel message!

God used my journey of participation in Al Anon greatly with me, in both practical and spiritual ways. If you are adversely affected by alcoholism in your family, His plan may be different for you, loved one, but each one needs to earnestly pray about where God could be leading you. What is good for one in God's plan could be harmful to another, so listen to *Him*. He custom makes our journeys! Do you know that? You must go wherever He leads *you*. Don't let anyone dissuade you once you believe you have heard from God. So guard your heart, and always pray for this spiritual leading. God does not use "one size fits all" remedies with His diverse beloved children. On the other hand, I will add that Jesus is *always* on the pathway.

In 2005 I am a newcomer to the Al Anon fellowship and it's concepts, but I find myself starting to hope that since the lost souls who started this program were believers, and that the fellowship sprung out of the founders' own divine remarkable spiritual experiences and healing, then I shall pursue participating. I'd been told about the fellowship after I had an emotional breakdown in my living room one night, and literally collapsed onto the floor with despair over my son's addiction, when he was about 25 years old. The mother of the mother of my grandchild recommended with kindness that I try attending, and handed me a brochure. (ironically this dear lady never seemed to benefit from it herself, at least during that time) I started to go to meetings regularly, three to four times a week and sometimes more. I gradually began to grasp the major principles presented. The major concept that redeems its worthiness to God's kingdom in my eyes is that it teaches we are powerless over *all things*, but to take heart, because our God is not. (and He has overcome the world John 16:33) Over and over throughout Al Anon's literature we read that "God is in control, not *you*." I found no struggle with the attendees there that failed to recognize the God of the bible as being their *only* higher power, because I knew that *if* God eventually opened their eyes and led them to truth and saved them by His grace, just like he did for me while I was still drowning in my transgressions, that they would eventually comprehend the truth. I rested in that hope, the fullness of the work of Jesus crucified and risen. He relentlessly pursues the ungodly! He meets us where we are at!

In ancient days did He not intervene powerfully in man's long established, man created superstitious pagan rituals of animal and human sacrifice carried out to appease, please, and worship their false gods? Humans of ancient days expected to benefit from the ascribed powers of these gods. Did God not meet mankind in their sinful practices, exactly where *these ancient people* were at, and over time transform their corrupt godless sacrificial rituals into something that actually *was* sacred when carried out *His* way? Did He not begin by divinely engineering the establishment of *sacrifice* as the *means* by which sin could be atoned for, by which people may be reconnected to their alienated and forgotten God? Can you see the link between God's intervening in man's chronic sinful practices, as He spoke through Moses to His people, and His using this sacrificial system as the foreshadowing of the very *Way* by which they might be reconciled to the one true Creator? He meets us collectively and individually, wherever we are at, in our sinful walks.

> "But if anybody does sin, we have one who speaks to the Father in our defense-Jesus Christ, the Righteous One. He is the atoning sacrifice for our sins, and not only for ours, but also for the sins of the whole world."
>
> (1 John 2:1-2 NIV)

We read in Genesis that God initially selected a special people of His very own to teach and to bless *first*, a stubborn "stiff necked" people, resistant to change, just like us. Through Abram (later called Abraham) God lets us all know that "all peoples on earth would be blessed" through His chosen Israelite nation. (Genesis 12:3) The point is that as we read God's word, we began to see more and more a characteristic of our sovereign God. He meets sinners *where they are at*. He *desires* that all become His children.

After attending Al Anon for a few more years and benefiting measurably, I decide that I will only stop partaking at these meetings if God clearly shows me at any time that He no longer wants me there, despite the fact my dear beloved pastor is opposed. I do not have a heart of rebellion but know for certain that we obey God, not men. God did eventually, years later, remove my desire and need to attend, letting me know I had learned what He wanted me to. He led me to other pastures. I have learned that a big part of trusting God *only*, in addictive messes, is by recalling daily that the same sovereign God who pulled *me* out of the pit, is also fully available to my son! God desires *even more than I do* that Jared be an eternal part of His spiritual family. I become built up over time in confidence that God *can* and *will* change him, just as He has changed and still does change me. I come to understand that God loves him *and died for him while he was yet still a sinner.* (us too) This means that I must *stop* striving to save him (be Jared's savior). I receive *and implement* the counsel to detach with love, and find my serenity in my faith, which assures me that my God is *more than able.* My Father also lovingly and regularly reminds me that I am *not able,* and I find great relief in that knowledge. I can *stop trying, and hand it over. I am not the Changer.*

I *can* pray, and *know* my loving Father hears me. "God have mercy upon me, a sinner." (Luke 18:13) This grace is sufficient.

I become determined to practice something new. I let go of trying to manage or facilitate Jared's recovery path to sobriety. I am now convinced that I am could be and probably am getting in the way of what our sovereign Lord is doing with him. I determine to remain detached from the chaos and agony, no matter how bad things look on the surface. *I am believing without doubting that God can do it. The Holy Spirit helps me to persist in this belief.*

Let go and let God.

Serenity comes to me by setting my face like a flint to practice this kind of faith, day by day.

Others in my co-dependent family and in the world may have judged me cold, heartless, misguided or unloving as I handed it *all* over, detached from the awfulness of it all, laid it all down at the foot of the cross. Yet, my decision rose out of belief in the greatest love in all existence...God's for us. Perhaps others thought I'd waited too long to do so. God actually had me in a place where other's opinions didn't matter much to me anymore. I continued to seek instruction in Godly wisdom. I was learning to seek to please *only* the Lord. This was a big stretch for me and still can be, considering the *people pleasing* piece of my sinful nature and the temporary reward I seem to love when people shower their approval on me. To trust God alone, be willing to live with the disapproval, criticism and sometimes demonization of others, some who mean much to me, goes against the grain of my flesh. It goes against the grain of my upbringing. I am saying here that *trusting God alone and completely at all times* "kicks against the goads" of my inherent sinful nature that continues to wage the warfare to rule in me! Satan wants me hopeless and anxious. Oh, the ongoing warfare.

> "He gives strength to the weary and increases the power
> of the weak. Even youths grow tired and weary, and
> young men stumble and fall; but those who hope in the
> Lord will renew their strength. They will soar on wings
> like eagles; they will run and not grow weary, they will
> walk and not be faint."
>
> (Isaiah 40:29-31)

One day, after Jared's repeat performance of disappearing from the home in order to break his sobriety and drink, I snap! I temporarily lose my sanity. Every new behavior I have been being coached in at Al Anon flies out the window! I do not care in *this* moment about the new behaviors I am supposed to be trying on for size, as far as keeping my own hands off and trusting my well equipped God. I do not care about keeping my own focus on my own relationship with God. I totally "lose it" emotionally and with a totally irrational mind driven by helplessness, anger, darkness, a mother's indignant fury and the angst and hopeless conviction of final defeat, I toss all reason aside and jump into my car. Yes, I'm sobbing again. I hope you are not too weary of my writing that, as this desperate painful helplessness has been the door through which God has poured so much of his love. Against much wiser council I have received, I am driving straight to Paxton and Peyton's house to pull my son out of that detestable filthy swamp of sin. I resemble in no way the father who waited, in Luke 15. In this moment of having lost all self control I don't really give a hoot if it's not considered a good choice. Whether or not I find him there, I shall express my anger and my hatred of everything those two men represent in the destruction of my son's life, by *spitting in their face. Yes, that is my actual intention and plan.* I am shaking from head to toe. I am determined to spit on them.

It's only a few miles, and I arrive there quickly and pull up in front of the house. All initially appears quiet. It is mid afternoon. I get out of the car and go up to the front door and pound on it. No answer. I pound more and ring the bell. Nothing. In frustration and defeat, I turn and head for my car. Then I hear a lawn mower. Peyton comes around the corner of the house pushing it.

I turn and face him. With all the venom and hatred I can muster from my inner being, I narrow my eyes and spit out the words "Is my son here?" At the same time I am thinking that this is my moment of truth...do I have enough hate inside of me to walk up to him and truly spit into his face? The trembling increases. I feel like I might fall over.

Peyton says that my son is not there, and that he doesn't know where he is. I hesitate as I contemplate what my next step is. It is time for me to act and follow through on my plan to spit in his face. I realize I can not do it. I don't have it in me to spit in an other's face. After a pregnant pause, I turn on my heel and stumble back to my car and get inside. I continue to fall further apart. I am blindly driving now. It is getting later on this Saturday afternoon. In my desperation, all that I can think of is that I need to get to an Al Anon meeting. I'm beyond despair. My need to be with other suffering hurting people who understand, who have walked with this brand of a mother's pain and unbearable loss, is overwhelming. No one else but other parents of sons and daughters contending with alcoholism and addiction will do. I can't think straight.

I can't think of where a Saturday evening Al Anon meeting is, where I know I will find the people I am desperate to be with on this night. The Saturday meeting I have always chosen this past year or so is scheduled in Peabody on Saturday mornings, so that's been over for hours. Somehow, I manage to make a call on my cell phone to an "800" number off of a brochure in my car, and beg the man who answers to direct me to an Al Anon meeting in the area. I tell him I'm in Salem (I'm driving randomly at this point) and he tells me there is one at a church fairly close to where I am, and gives me directions. These are the days prior to GPS. I am too upset to listen to him well, but although I'm not totally clear on the directions, I feel certain I can find the church.

I CAN'T FIND THE CHURCH!! I have a single driving purpose within, propelling me to find that church or die in my sorrows. I have given up all hope in my own ability to uplift the destinies of Jared, Bridget, and Tyler and set them on a fruitful path. I stop at several churches and investigate them to see if I can locate the usual posted signs meant to direct folks to which door to enter for the meetings. No signs. I decide to take the name from one church that could, in my estimation, be the one that offers the meeting tonight.

47

I call directory service for the number of their rectory, and leave an inquiry. I do this, and when no one answers I leave a desperate message on voicemail that sounds something like this "Hi my name is Melody and I'm calling to ask if you have an Al Anon meeting at your church tonight. Please please if anyone gets this message will you call me back so I will wait around if there is going to be a meeting." I left my cell number, then started driving again.

Minutes later, my cell rang. I grabbed for it as if it was my last hope.

"Hello is this Melody?" a male voice says.

"Yes this is me."

"Melody, this is Father Tim calling you back. Where are you right now? You sound very upset."

I told him that I was driving around the neighborhood of his church in Salem. He gently instructed me to pull over to the side of the road and park so that we could talk. I did so. When he was then assured that I was not going to drive into a wall due to my severe duress, he began to talk to me.

"Melody, there is no Al Anon meeting at our church. I can't believe that I'm even speaking with you. I'm in Boston right now, standing on a sidewalk. I'm supposed to be meeting some people. I had this funny feeling I should call the church and collect my messages just now. (years later I understood this is one way the Spirit works) I got yours, which was the only one on it. With no pen or paper to write your number down, I just picked up a small stone and scratched your number onto the side of a brick building so I wouldn't forget it. You and I are going to have our own Al Anon meeting right now together, if that's okay with you."

"Oh, thank you thank you so much for calling me!" I replied. With his encouragement and willingness to listen, I then blurted out the details of the events of my day, and my despair over the course of my son's life and those whose lives were being dreadfully harmed, in addition to his own. I told him how close to the end of my rope I was, how desperately I needed help. He listened with patience and love, and then shared the following.

"Melody, I just want to tell you how amazing it is to me that I got your phone message tonight. I never call to pick up my messages at the church on a Saturday night. My twin sister suffered with advanced alcoholism. My parents and I tried for years and years to save her, and we could not do it. She died of it several years ago. During those awful times when I was despairing, I learned to do something that I would like you to try. I would visualize my sick sister in my mind, and I would tenderly and with great love gently wrap her up in a soft, warm, beautiful blanket. I finally accepted I could not personally make her well. Then I would take my twin sister, wrapped up in that soft warm cozy comforting blanket, and I would hold her out and I would hand her up and pass her over, with both of my hands to the Lord, to hold. I want you to do that with your son. I want you to go through through that visual in your mind, and lovingly wrap Jared in that blanket, and hand him to the Lord. "

My mind was spinning, my thoughts were racing. I was breathless. It was so clear to me that this very moment on the phone with Father Tim, with tears streaming down my face as I listened to his calming words, was a divine appointment. The Lord knows how to link us to *exactly* the right person for the moment. Years later I can look back and recall the solace and comfort of Christ our Lord that I was given though him, Father Tim, all because he followed the prompting of the Holy Spirit within as he walked down a street carrying out other plans of his own, in Boston. This is what Lindsay Lyons was going to do the following year. (Chapter 4) Mostly, I was once again filled up with hope which had been direly absent from my heart all day. I was restored to sanity in those moments, my agony extinguished, not by my own efforts or striving but by the activity and orchestrations of my sovereign loving Father who created me, and made me his for all eternity.

Sometime later, perhaps weeks or months, I found out that there is no Al Anon meeting in Salem, MA on Saturday evenings. None. To this day there isn't one. It became obvious to me that the man who told me that there was, had done so in divine error. An oxymoron for sure.

> "The Lord is close to the brokenhearted and saves those who are crushed in spirit."
>
> Psalm 34:18 (NIV)

> "The Lord will rescue his servants; no one who takes refuge in him will be condemned."
>
> Psalm 34:22 (NIV)

CHAPTER SIX

"And we know that in all things God works for the good of those who love him, who have been called according to his purpose."

Romans 8:28 (NIV)

"We are not trying to please men, but God, who tests our hearts."

1 Thessalonians 2:4 (NIV)

"In this you greatly rejoice, though now for a little while you may have had to suffer grief in all kinds of trails. These have come so that your faith-of greater worth than gold, which perishes even though refined by fire-may be proved genuine and may result in praise, glory and honor when Jesus Christ is revealed."

1 Peter 1:6-7 (NIV)

IT IS EARLY IN THE YEAR 2007 and I am living alone in a lovely apartment in Swampscott, MA. I'm fifty four years old. I continue to work as a nurse at Brigham and Women's Hospital in Boston, and still do much recreational running in my off time. I live not far from the ocean, where I have a favorite six mile running course along the beautiful shoreline from Swampscott to Nahant and back. I remain single and living an independent life since my second divorce 15 years before.

At this time I am still licking my lingering emotional wounds from my last serious failed relationship with a man. Four years ago Andrew (name changed) had asked me to marry him and given me an engagement ring that he had custom designed for me by a local jeweler. It seemed like a dream come true. A large portion of my focus in life up to now had been to find the perfect partner, and receiving a gorgeous ring to top off the promise was a sad and shallow dream of mine. I shake my head as I recall vividly some of my skewed worldly beliefs that remained with me for some time after salvation. I wasn't a materialistic person, and had zero interest in marrying a man for money, but had believed the lie touted in worldly women's magazines I used to read- that a large shiny diamond indicated that a man *must* love me more. I was thrilled initially, but then deeply wounded when he rapidly backed out of the proposal after a couple of weeks! This was due to the objection of two of his adult sons, and two of his deceased wife's friends who had never been willing to open their hearts to me, and had acted rather meanly. The two women had been hostile to me since the beginning. The two of Andrew's four grown children who had quickly talked Andrew out of what he yearned to do seemed to have not finished with their own grieving process for their mother, who had died a few years before I met their dad. Andrew lacked backbone, and in the end I have no doubt that it turned out to be a good thing for me.

I myself was not terribly empathetic with the adult children's objections, and thought they were self centered and oblivious to their dad's needs and desire to go through his life with a woman he adored. I had not yet lost parent of my own. I was firmly convinced his boys who were grown men, should be "ready" for their dad's life to move on. I was unable to relate to their tight hold on their father. I judged them as selfish. I eventually was able to forgive them for their inability to see their dad move forward and be joyful in his deep happiness with me, but that occurred years later. Andrew himself remained willingly in their grip of ownership and control, enmeshed, and gave up the woman he loved to please *them*. His daughter told a good friend of mine several years later that her dad remained very depressed over his decision. As the Lord slowly healed my heart, much of this pain being my own fault since I'd willingly chosen while dating him to remain a carnal Christian- allowing physical intimacy in the relationship- I had to come to understand that the Lord had ultimately used their rejection and Andrew's weakness for my protection. He often does with us. Did you ever hear the phrase that "sometimes people's rejection is actually the Lord's protection?"

I had made many mistakes of my own in trying to force my yearned for outcome-my life long goal of marriage to a functional good partner. Believing I did not want to live without him, I attempted to engineer it happening from my own strength and will. After much heartache I *finally* saw and realized in hindsight that this union had not been God's will for me. I had fought too hard for the relationship, for my own will, instead of recognizing and trusting in the Lord's leading. I had my eyes *not* on Jesus but on Andrew! It caused me unnecessary grief. I stubbornly pursued my own plan to win him back against his sons' and two merciless female friend's wills. I was certain I could convince Andrew that he could get past his need for a stamp of approval from others, and that if he stood his ground that the others would come around. False idols were influencing choices on both parts. His- for across the board approval from family and friends; mine-being consumed with yearning too much for a marriage that worked, creating an idol. Neither one of those things granted can ever make a person whole. I convinced myself that Andrew would eventually see his error, and that I had the power to convince him of it. I was wrong.

For awhile after the initial break up he visited me secretly now and then, and I was foolishly *too* patient with his indecisiveness. He took me out to dinner at places that he was confident we would not be seen. I was finally able to see the lack of dignity, respect and nobility in that-allowing myself to be with a man who felt he needed to see me on the sly.

Anyhow, all of these things, and without doubt many more, had been the cause of our broken engagement a few years earlier. The dear man simply was not equipped to disappoint or go against his children or two controlling women friends who were clearly consumed with jealousy and unwilling to adjust to me, in any way.

Truth be told, Andrew drank way too much scotch every evening! I could have never been happy with that. He seemed to bow down to and seek to associate with people with money and worldly social status. I really am turned off by that. He encouraged me to give up my lovely home in Topsfield and rent a room in a friend's house that was much closer to him, "just for a few months just until we're married." I did that! In retrospect I see what a complete fool I was! Ladies, please listen! As a consequence of my awful choices and of not consistently seeking God's will, I eventually had no home to call my own, and no husband, either. This is *not* what God wants for us.

I am so grateful to God today that as I look back on this period of my life I can see that he had grown me enough that I could not live with a man I wasn't married to. I could no longer willingly go *that* far in displeasing my God. I can see there was at least *some* change in me, though not much. Andrew was more than willing to follow his kids' advice and just "live together."No, thank you. Other than experiencing that check in my spirit, albeit I was sinning in many other ways, I would have convinced myself to "just move in." Believe me, I do not mean to sound righteous when I write that because I was behaving as if I *were* married to him in our relationship! I felt helpless at the time to leave him, and often stayed at his home on the weekends. I would not *walk away from the hope I had found in him, Andrew.*

If this sounds wrong to you, it is! It is always the wrong place to attach hope to-a *person.* We should never ever attach hope in a horizontal direction in this fallen corrupted world, to a created thing. That's a big mistake, guaranteed to lead to bitterness, depression, and spiritual poverty! Genuine, real hope comes only when we focus vertically on Jesus. So many of us of us tend to make this large error! People can not deliver and satisfy what we ultimately are searching for in our innermost being, and need and yearn to worship. Can you see the divided heart in me in my tragic story? We can not serve two masters, sisters. We can not serve both our selves as master, and our God too. It is good for us to decide once and for all into *what* we will place our *hope* in for the remainder of our lives-into the hands of the Creator, our Father- and live as He tells us to-or will we keep looking to created things- people for instance, who all eventually fail us in one way or another. (there's forgiveness for that) Hope in Jesus will *never* disappoint.

I was struggling in 2007 for final healing and closure of this heart breaking fruitless and disastrous romance, and to somehow erase completely the bitter sadness of knowing that this man would not be becoming my husband. He would not be the one who would fulfill my dream of being a good wife to a good man. The year the relationship had begun with him was very early on during my carnal infant years of being drawn towards the Lord, and while I was just beginning to learn about what it meant to walk with Him.

I had made the grave and damaging mistake of engaging in a sexual union with Andrew. Yes girls and ladies, let me assure you as one who was buying into everything that our mainstream culture taught regarding sexuality, at that time of my life, that the results of *not* following God's ways for our good and protection can and *will* shatter you. You see, when you make this choice to sleep with a man and act on it, sexual intercourse will *bind* you ever so much more deeply to him. This can be so wonderful and is such a sweet part of God's way! Yet, this way is intended as part of His design and blessings for *marriage*. Sexual pleasure, closeness and joy serve the marriage bond and build that special intimacy that a man and his wife share and treasure just between themselves. It's a gift of marriage, a blessing, and when we receive it it gives us satisfaction and pleasure. God has beautiful purposes for it, and it acts as a glue, strengthening the family unit.

Only for the purpose that I may more fully share my testimony with you, dear reader, I want to emphasize that if you unwisely engage in sex with men that have not devoted themselves to your best interests and to be *your* committed husband, that you will set yourself up for suffering that need not be. Ladies *please listen to me.* I have lived the pain of which I write. When you choose sexual union with a man you are not married to, it will drastically elevate the heart pain of being wrenched away from an intimate bonding of the marital kind if the relationship fails. It took so much longer for my heart pain to subside than it might have, had I adhered to Godly wisdom and relied on my heavenly Father for self control. If you are one of God's chosen daughters and still a virgin when you marry, then you will be giving your husband a priceless gift that he will treasure. If that is not possible, don't despair, but don't be like I foolishly was! I lied to myself that since I was already experienced from marriage (or otherwise), that abstinence no longer mattered.

That is a lie from hell. It does, and greatly! Many might think it silly, even ridiculous, to abstain from the pleasures of physical intimacy later in life when one has already been sexually active beforehand. I can assure you from my own experience that it isn't. Applying Godly wisdom, honoring Him, will *never* fail you. Let that man that won't wait walk away.

Men are different that we are, not as fragile, and are able to walk away from those they have had sex with without the same level of heart upheaval and damage. I had not understood this principle of why the Lord makes it so, at the time; why He tells women to preserve themselves for the marital relationship, and thus I found myself yearning for restoration well after I could have moved on after Andrew. I had not been wise. I had trusted a person more than I trusted the soundness of Godly boundaries. This elongated pain was a consequence of my being selective in my obedience to the Lord's commands in the earlier years of being saved, and of prioritizing my pleasure and will over His. There's always a cost. Sin has consequences. The Father's commands are meant to protect His beloved daughters.

Do not despair, it can take time, often years, to be deprogrammed from years of worldly conditioning and buying into secular lies. The Lord will bring you through any lingering guilt remnants stemming from a sinful sexual past. His perspective is the *only* one that counts for eternity. He will make you spiritually whole, purified, *just as if you'd never sinned.* He *will* do it for the asking.

Very early the next year, in 2008, I had met very nice, impressive, intelligent, and very kind man on a blind date that keenly sparked my interest. He was a snowbird living in Florida for the winter. After two meetings with him while he was home in Massachusetts for business reasons (one in January and one early February), I'd heard nothing from him. I had pretty much forgotten about him, and had also become completely distracted away from caring about a dating life, by a medical episode that was around the corner, which I shall share with you. (Curt informed me later that he'd also been diverted during this time by an unexpected trip to Israel). We'd had only had two "meetings", thus it was not yet an actual relationship. More like just an "acquaintance of interest". I married Curt a year and a half later! We remain together to this day, and he is the guy for me, second only to Jesus.

Despite no relationship or potential mate on the horizon in 2007, life does this year seem pretty good to me overall. I have good friends. My life feels balanced. I attend a wonderful non-denominational, growing, bible based church led by a young energetic gifted pastor Matthew Nadworny, who is on *fire* for the Lord. (by this time the Lord had moved me to North Shore Calvary Chapel) I continue to be a seeker of God's truth and wisdom, albeit a slow learner. I do recall that that was the time period (2007- 2008) that I read "Hinds Feet on High Places "by Hurnard (a favorite of my deceased older sister Jan) ; "Facing Your Giants" by Lucado ; "Why Grace Changes Everything" and "Living Water" by Chuck Smith; and "The Hiding Place" by Corrie Ten Boom-along with many other similar books written by believing followers of Christ, heroes and heroines of the faith. I continue to attend a Calvary Chapel Christian Woman's retreat every fall with my sister Diane and my mom, who became a believer after my dad's passing, and together we worship and feed on Christ. I'm in the word a *lot*. I can't get enough. I am so spiritually thirsty! I listen to Christian radio on my way into and on my way home from work, a one and a half to two hour commute each way. Chuck Swindoll is a favorite, and the program "Focus on the Family," and Dr. J Vernon McGee. Others, too. I played all of Elisabeth Elliot's CD's several times over. Gone were my days of looking for truth in all the wrong places! God finally had me gleaning truth from trustworthy sources, His written word being foremost. My ladder has been shifted to a different wall. God is kneading me, changing me, using all things working together.

On December 8, 1996, my precious older sister Janice had succumbed at the young age of 47 to breast cancer. She'd battled it for thirteen years before she died and went home to be with the Lord. She was the pioneer in my family who became "born again" before many of us in my family followed suit, in the Lord's perfect timing. I chuckle and shake my head when I think of how my unbelieving mother and I used to feel sorry for Jan that she had turned into a "bible thumper" and we would talk *about* her over the phone. Her *own mother and sister* wagging our evil tongues! (James 3:5-6). *What a pitiful memory.* We'd agree with one another that it was quite obvious that the only reason that Jan needed this radical belief system and was clinging to, preaching God, and studying the bible constantly was because she was so despairing due to her awful and terminal disease. If not for that, we reasoned in our unsaved minds together (an extremely dangerous activity), she would have never bought all this "religious" belief stuff hook, line and sinker. She *needed* it for comfort...poor Jan! We felt *so bad* for her both for her terminal diagnosis of cancer, *and* for her apparently needing to find comfort and hope in God. Little were we aware that our own terminal spiritual diagnosis's were incomparably deadly, compared to what she had. *She was the one* to whom life had been *imparted by Christ, not us!* We were the ones on a road, at that time, to eternal spiritual death and separation from God *and we did not know it.* *(except for His kind mercies which were revealed in our lives years later)*

As for me, even after my beloved older sister and childhood mentor Janice died, I had little concern for myself regarding potentially ever receiving a diagnosis of cancer. It just wasn't going to be anything that was going to happen to me, as far as I was concerned. On the other hand, my younger sister Diane had great concerns that she explained stemmed from the fact that her twin daughters Kate and Kelley were still just little girls, only three years old, and she felt she needed to do all within her power to insure and increase the likelihood that she would be alive and present to raise them. Her main fear on this was her thought that perhaps as Jan's sisters we might be carrying the gene that was guaranteed to eventually cause breast cancer and premature death. We'd had a paternal aunt that died of the same. Diane chose to pursue the genetic testing with the idea in mind that if she carried the gene, she would undergo a double radical mastectomy prophylactically. Her testing came back negative for the troublesome gene. (Years later she was diagnosed with mesothelioma, another amazing story of God's working in the lives of those He gave to Christ)

As for me, I was unconcerned and unafraid. I was confident I would not get cancer of any kind, and maintained a casual, cavalier, and unworried attitude on this matter. I ignored my younger sister's suggestions that I be proactive and pursue the genetic testing. I'd felt no need. In the years that ensued after Jan's passing, I *never* thought about getting cancer at all! I confess did not even get regular mammograms. (yes me, the nurse) That's where I was coming from in my emotional thought life. Cancer was *not* on my personal worry list.

So, out of the nineties and back to the year 2008 now, when one morning in March I woke up from an extremely vivid and realistic dream. I found myself still brimming with the emotions of fear and dread that it had provoked within. I had been diagnosed with cancer in that dream! The upsetting, deep disturbing feelings lingered in my mind as my morning unfolded, and it took me many hours to shake them off.

At the end of that same week on Friday evening, I was at home alone, in my Swampscott apartment. My gynecologist, Dr. Shaak, called me with the results of a yearly pap smear, the routine annual test women undergo to rule out *cervical* cancer. I had not given that routine visit a second conscious thought. She made it clear that she was quite stunned that this test had revealed cancerous cells in my *uterus*, because the test was never considered a means to screen for uterine or ovarian cancer. (in 2013 this started to be explored for that specific usage, and as of this current date is not used) She kept saying to me on the phone "Melody you just don't know how lucky you are that the pathologist picked this up, we just don't detect uterine cancer this way! The pathologist that looked at your slide is extremely gifted to have seen it."

To any reader who has been initiated into this special club, the "I now have cancer club", I have no doubt that you recall vividly the myriad of emotions that follow your diagnosis. What a hard passage it is. With initial diagnosis your sense of well being and the continuation of your physical life hang in the balance, and one feels overwhelmed by all of the unknowns. The turning on a dime of your whole certainty of continued physical existence is enormously difficult to come to terms with. When things seem to be going well we all seem to live with a false illusion of being in control! Ha! What a reality check! In addition to my own struggle with fears of mortality, but mostly fears of of the potential suffering in some unknown battle that would lead up to ultimately facing that, I felt so very, very alone. I had no husband to help me. Who was going to help me? My mother was still alive, but I was determined not to burden her with this truth. She was doing really well at seventy nine and she even still worked part time. She was finally thriving in her new life after the passing of my dad several years earlier. I did not want to upset her with what I knew would be staggering news-after all, she'd already buried one daughter who had succumbed to cancer. My son was submerged in alcoholism in New York City. I remember I placed a needy call to my sweet and dear friend Claire Turner on that evening after I hung up from receiving Dr. Shaak's grim diagnosis. I will always remember and be grateful for how kind, reassuring and supportive she was.

A few mornings later after receiving my life changing news, while still reeling with the shock, I recalled that I had signed up to facilitate two Al Anon meetings over the next two weeks! One on a Wednesday evening in Peabody, and one on a Monday night in Salem. My first thought was that I simply needed to cancel both commitments. After all...I had CANCER! How could I possibly speak effectively when I didn't even know if I was going to live or die? Poor me! I *had* to cancel. Surely there was no other choice.

A few days later, and before I had canceled anything, I felt the Lord speak softly and gently to my heart. He told me that while I was thinking that I was incapable to speak publicly while in my duress, and that my messages would be rendered weak and ineffective because I was so distraught while waiting for my continued work up and surgery, that He was going to use *exactly* those circumstances to speak to others through me. That's amazing Lord, I told Him. You are going to use this evil disease for your purposes? So the Lord changed my mind from backing out of speaking at the meetings, to giving me a yearning to do so.

"Maybe they will listen to me a little more intently *because* I have cancer Lord?" I asked. Is this not typical of our human nature? When a person has something that seems radically awful going on do we not tend to pay a little more attention to what they say and do? I might as well use my status for some noble intention! Maybe they will perceive me with more *interest* because I am in a vulnerable state, do not know where this is all going, and they will feel a bit sorry for me. Maybe it will *perk up their ears* when I use the horrifying "cancer card!"Why not? Had not the Lord put that card in my hand? Not to manipulate by my own thought out plan and engineering, but to pursue obediently what *He was orchestrating to unfold.* I was made to understand that whether I was cured or whether I died, that this opportunity may never come again-to speak to a group of folks prior to my surgery, without any confidence that I would be cured, and prior to knowing my final prognosis. I was to speak from this position of being in "no man's land", and while still frightened! "What message would you want to give using my mouth, Lord?"

"TRUST."

Trust? "YES. DO YOU?"

I'm scared.

"DO YOU TRUST ME WITH YOUR SON?"

Yes. You have been teaching me to do that.

"IS THERE A REASON YOU WOULD TRUST ME WITH YOUR SON BUT NOT TRUST ME WITH YOUR CANCER?"

Oh. You gave me the dream a few days *before* I had my diagnosis to let me see your Hand in this? To reassure me and create in me a confidence that You have not abandoned me?

"YES. GO AND SPEAK TO THE PEOPLE I WILL HAVE THERE, AND TELL THEM HOW YOU TRUST ME NO MATTER WHAT. NO MATTER WHAT. NO MATTER HOW FRIGHTENED OR ANXIOUS YOU ARE, AND EVEN THOUGH YOU CAN'T SEE WHERE ANY OF THIS IS GOING...WITH YOUR SON, OR WITH THIS CANCER I HAVE ALLOWED FOR YOU. IF YOU TELL THEM NOW, WHEN YOU DON'T KNOW IF YOU WILL BE HEALED, THE MESSAGE WILL BE MORE POWERFUL. TELL THEM TO TRUST ME NO MATTER WHAT."

You will have to give me the courage and make the words come, Lord. You will have to hold me up.

And so I went.

The first night that I went to the Wednesday night meeting on the second floor of The Knights of Columbus to keep my promise to speak, I had jotted down some notes to refer to about my faith in God, how it had began, and how it had continued to grow over the years. The room was full. Somehow the Lord put words in my mouth to tie my current faith in God in my particular situation, and *how it calmed and comforted me*, together with the collective plights and heartbreak and mourning in the room. *"No matter what we see, no matter what seems to be happening, let's trust our God. Faith in Him is the only thing that will help us! It is the only answer to everything that happens to us!"* Let me assure you that these rooms at these kinds of meetings overflow with broken despairing hearts. Feelings of helplessness and distress flourish within the attendees, whose lives have become horrifyingly unmanageable by the impact of the sins of their own and their family's humanity. This refers not only to the addicted, but also to *all* of us spared from that particular affliction! Do not deceive yourself that your sin is any less lethal, prettier or cleaner than that of addicts' my friend. Sin is sin.

Would we not all have perfect peace if we could fully comprehend the character of our God? Yet we experience lives and pain that often feel unbearable, and leave us reeling in agony. We find no rest! Whether watching a beloved one become more and more destroyed and distanced from what God is able to make them to be, by their bondage to an addictive substance, or reckoning with fright and shock caused by one's own devastating frightening diagnosis, the agonizing feelings that are elicited by either scenario are deep. They can only be soothed by an innate belief in a God who is sovereign, and wastes *nothing* in the lives of His children. To know

Him is to have *hope*. To trust Him is to know serenity by finding rest *in Him* -whether or not our diseases are cured or our loved ones sober up- or, whether they or we die. As Shadrach, Meshach and Abednego replied to King Nebuchadnezzar before being tossed into the blazing furnace "the God we serve is able to save us from it but *even if He does not we will not worship or serve idols".(paraphrased from Dan 3:17, 18)* Oh, to have a faith like theirs! Every single event that happens in our lives, loved ones, can be used to bring us to entry into true faith in the God of the bible, or to deepen that amount of faith which He has orchestrated in us already. Believe! Peace is possible, regardless of the apparent circumstances-because the Source of your peace is not dependent on the circumstances, and able to change them at will. But one must believe and TRUST that no matter what things *appear to be* from our drastically, vastly limited human vision and perspective, that our all knowing and loving Creator *knows* what He is doing in and with His children's lives. It is *always for our good and always to bring Him glory. Believe!* Ask Jesus, God, to bring you to it. All that happens *to you* is *for you*.

I know in my heart and deepest soul that there were those that received a message from the Lord through what He sent me to say at Al Anon that Wednesday night. Perhaps it was only one who heard, or maybe it was more than one that were His intended recipients. It's not important for me to know, it is only important to sow. The only significant action on my part was choosing to obey the promptings of the Holy Spirit. One man did come up to me and expressed overwhelming gratitude for the message after my first night speaking. The Lord had given him ears to hear for sure. Maybe on the other side of eternity I shall find out if the Lord had targeted more than that one guy. Would not our Lord have chosen to die on the cross for you even if *you* were the *only one* that required salvation from what you are, from the wickedly deceitful heart you were born with, and provided a way, *one Way*, for reconciliation to the Father? He would have. Do you know that? *Believe!* Knock on the door of heaven with all of your doubts and all of your hesitation and all of your cynicism. I tell you to expect an answer from heaven even though you may now find this "silly."The motive that God sees in your heart must be right. He must see a sincere and pure hunger for the truth. It is He who will do the work and will build your faith.

In a nutshell, the summary of my delivered message those two nights speaking at Al Anon was "If I can now trust our God to be in control of ALL things (and I do), and if ALL means ALL...then I can and will trust him with the destiny of my beloved son. I have and am receiving immeasurable comfort by trusting Him with mine, while I wait to find out what my medical prognosis will be after my surgery. Do you see that I am alright? It's not because of me. If I can be made alright in my fear and in my cancer crisis then you can be made alright too, while you wait on God to work with your beloved sick one. You can do it but only with God's help. Be encouraged!"

You see, if we say we trust the Lord and simultaneously our lives unfold uneventfully without all sorts of trials, tribulations and crisis's-then our trust is never put to the test, deepened, or Godly character refined in us. How do we know we *do* trust if we don't get a chance to put it into actual practice? To call our verbalized and mentally thought out ,inwardly experienced trust into action? To test our proclaimed trust? If we say "I'm sure I can jump that hurdle" and then we never get an opportunity to jump-how do we develop confidence that we *can?* This is *again* why James tells us to "count it all as joy." This is why Paul tells us we "can do all things through Christ who strengthens us". The outcome to believing and *applying* these words of scripture is an unshakable faith. All while acknowledging our own weakness and inability! You will grow in faith by drinking willingly and trustingly from *whatever* cup the

Lord gives to you to drink. You will know that you *can't, on your own, but He can, if you die to your fleshly weakness and inability and let Him work through you. Christ's strength is imparted to His beloved!* Give Him your "death" in every moment and He will give you His life! Become a living sacrifice! It is He who lovingly holds your golden chalice as you accept the divine brew within, which has been so lovingly prepared. Satan is only a tool for our Almighty God to use to grow His children into mature saints. That is a promise directly from our Lord. He *has overcome.*

"Why are you downcast O my soul? Why so disturbed within me? Put your hope in God, for yet I will praise him, my Savior"

Psalm 42:5 (NIV)

"But as for you, you meant evil against me; but God meant it for good, in order to bring it about as *it is this day* to save many people alive."

Genesis 50:20 (NKJV)

"I have told you these things, so that in me you may have peace. In this world you will have trouble. But take heart! I have overcome the world."

John 16:33 (NIV)

"Now faith is being certain of what we hope for and certain *of what we do not see.*"

Hebrews 11:1
(NIV, emphasis by author)

CHAPTER SEVEN

"It shall come to pass, that in the place where it was said
unto them, ye are not my people, there it shall be said
unto them, ye are the sons of the living God."

Hosea 1:10 (KJV)

"For God did not give us a spirit of timidity, but a spirit
of power, of love and of self-discipline."

2 Timothy 1:7 (NIV)

✝ TAIYE OZIGBO IS A WONDERFUL and extraordinary African
American woman who grew up in Nigeria. I was blessed to
work with her for some amount of years early in the 2000's at
Brigham and Women's Hospital in Boston, before she moved to
Texas with her family. She was the full time medical assistant for
our department at Brigham and Women's Asthma, Allergy and
Immunology ambulatory care department. That's where I was a
nurse for the last (almost) 18 years of my active medical career.

I will never forget the sound of her rich, earthy voice, dripping
and resonating with its Nigerian accent, or forget the manner in
which she spoke with confidence, authority and boldness when
speaking about that which she believed in and trusted. To this
day, whenever I hear a woman with a similar accent speak, my
heart is lifted up with nostalgic and loving memories of Taiye. I
felt a nobility and soundness emanate from her spirit, which drew

me to her. In retrospect I will say the Jesus within her was a magnet to me.

She chose to be a loving and supportive encouragement to me during the years we worked together, especially the last few before she moved. I don't know the reasons why the Lord put it on her heart to reach out to me to extend comfort and encouragement during my times of undisguised distress, but I do know that He used her as yet another one to show me that He is present, and often works through others He has placed around us to speak to us, and to teach.

There was more than one day, I don't recall how many, that I had come into work unable to conceal my reactive distress and despair over my son's progressive alcoholism, at least not from those who knew me. There was much ongoing tribulation in his and other's lives, including mine, rooted in his disease of human weakness and sin, alcoholism. It was agonizing to watch. Taiye showed me great compassion and a willingness to come alongside and help me carry this burden. She would sometimes talk with me about this ongoing trial in my life, and I have no doubt that the Lord prompted her at the perfect times to do so. It was during these kind of conversations that we quickly discovered that we both had hearts that were full on for Jesus. We both really trusted in the Lord. Of course, that drew us much closer to one another and fanned the flame of sisterly love.

One day Taiye entered my office in her bold and rooted in Godly confidence way, brimming over with assurance that she had something of the utmost importance to reveal to me. She announced to me that the Lord had given her a dream the very previous night while sleeping, regarding my son. Have you ever listened to a believing and confident African woman speak about that which she is certain of? It leaves little room for doubt as you listen! I could not have asked or hoped for a finer delivery or a finer deliverer of the Lord's message regarding my son on that day.

I can still hear her voice now. "I had a dream about your son! Melody, your son *is going to be alright! He is going to be fine. Do not doubt it! When I have this kind of dream and the Lord shows me things, it is always true. Always. I saw your son walking into a church. He went down into the front, deep into the church, and the people started lifting him up. They lifted him up over their heads and passed him along to one another and he was held high above their heads. In this dream I was shown that your son Jared is going to be just fine, and you need to to believe it! Your son is going to be alright, I am telling you, your son is going to be ALRIGHT!"* Her confidence and her assurance in the truth of her words was unmistakable.

It is now the following summer, July, 2006. Taiye had taken to giving me a call at home from time to time, to check in on me. I lived alone at this time. I immensely enjoyed chatting with her. I believe she must have had an innate sense of the duress that I was under during this season of my life. There was much ongoing loss. Hope for my son's life to turn around to sustained sobriety was hanging by a thread at best; I'd intentionally left my son and his girlfriend and their precious baby behind to live together minus me in the condo that I had foolishly purchased with Jared, in order to allow their relationship to die a natural death minus my interfering "help" and enabling (knowing it would lead to a foreclosure and credit ruined); I was living in a temporary home, renting an apartment up the street from them so I could be available to babysit. Living in a transitional home with that feeling of "not-for-long" was very *contrary* to my own need of stability in a home; my loyal beautiful German shepherd Anka, who seemed to have be the one steady reliable living presence and companion in my life for thirteen constant years had died; and a major love relationship (previously mentioned) hadn't worked out. That pain and disappointment lingered. The man (Andrew, from a previous chapter) was seeing someone else, which added to the aching of my heart.

On this summer day I was up at Lake Winnepausakee in New Hampshire for the weekend at my cousin Eva's cabin, struggling with my broken heart, and with my pitifully sad inability to come to terms with my self desire and will not being fulfilled. I'm not sure if I called Taiye or if she called me on that day, but I clearly remember exactly where I was standing in order to try and get a decent connection so I could hear Taiye speak to me on my little silver flip top cell phone. We were talking about the man who had rejected *me* in the end, and she was giving me her viewpoint and thoughts which truly intrigued me, regarding this man, and the complex psychological factors that seemed to inhibit and control him. She emphasized that God had showed her that the man loved me very much but there was "something about him" that he just could not overcome, in order to make the decision to be with me in marriage.

Like a little broken helpless bird without wings who can't help itself, I believe I craved hearing these thoughts from her in order to validate in my mind what I believed to be true, that I was indeed loved. My need to hear her consoling version seemed a pitiful but *only* alternative to the fact that he was unequipped or just unwilling to vocalize much of what was going on on his end of things to me. I was so bewildered that he had chosen separation from me when I was still so convinced of his deep caring. I persisted pathetically in trying to understand his choice, and could not.

She told me something during this conversation that I found

quite odd, really strange. She said "Melody I can't say how I know this, but I just *know* it. There has been a HUGE secret in his family for a long time, something that you were never told, and that has been kept from you-and it has to do with his deceased wife. It is very significant. It's a *big* secret that has been kept for a long time."She did not claim to know what the secret was, just that it existed. I didn't think much more about what she said, as I had no idea whether there was anything to it, or not. It just seemed weird that Taiye had said that to me, while at the same time intriguing. She was not one given to silly imaginings or speculations. I swear if anyone other than Taiye had said something to me like that I would have been convinced that they were "off their rocker". I put what she had said about there being a long kept secret on the back burner of my mind, and it never really came to mind again until a year or two later.

A year or two later I was at work one day and received an e-mail from a young woman named Meredith (name changed), the adult daughter of this back and forth again man that I had been engaged to, that had crushed my heart. He had three sons, two natural and one adopted, and also this one daughter, who was the youngest. We got along very well. She asked me in this email if her father had ever shared anything with me during the years we were together regarding the fact he was *not* her biological father! She was in her late twenties at the time. Apparently, she had just recently found out that she was, in reality, the biological offspring of a man her mother had had a brief affair with in the earlier years of of her marriage to Andrew. She had grown up believing all along that Andrew was her father. He *was* the person that had acted as a father, and willingly brought her up and loved her very much, along with the three boys. Meredith was struggling to integrate and reconcile this new startling new information about her birth father with her perception of who she was! She was rattled. She was seeking more details from those who were likely to know more, and thought I could be one of them. No, I responded to her-it was a family secret I had never been told.

Taiye's former prophetic disclosure to me via my little flip top cell phone, clearly revealed to her by the Holy Spirit and revealed to me by God through her with His good purpose in mind, was perfectly true! A *large family secret regarding the deceased wife of Andrew had been long hidden.*

Had Taiye spoken anything *else* to me that was also going to prove to be truth? A communication to me from God Himself?

I clearly recalled her assuring words a few years before, when she'd shared her vivid dream about Jared with me at work.

❋   ❋   ❋

It did not become clear to me until seven years later (in 2013) *why* the Lord had spoken to me through Taiye, using her to reveal *two* specific things, not just *one*. Both pieces of information should have been, according to human comprehension of how knowledge is obtained, unknowable to her. For certain the Lord had shown her something, and put it on her heart to share with me in 2006, regarding the "big long kept secret having to do with Meredith's mother". Obviously *that* was the generally unknown details of Meredith's biological conception. I believe with my whole being that the Lord revealed this to me using Taiye as His deliverer, to prepare and affirm to me that I was to trust her *formerly* conveyed information. I believe that the Lord was whispering to me, telling me to place great faith into believing the *other prophetic* message, the one regarding her dream that my son would be saved. He would be *alright.* He would be saved in a church and through people in a church that God would use. Lifted *up.* Can you see it?

Let me assure the reader that the social circles of Taiye and Andrew had *never* crossed, and that they lived in communities very far apart. She lived in a suburb of Boston actual, he in the bedroom community of Marblehead, over forty miles away. Even within his community, only a select few intimate family friends were aware of Meredith's's actual genetic parentage. Taiye had no comprehensible way of knowing there was a "secret" regarding Meredith's mother's brief affair during which Margaret was conceived, or that my former boyfriend Andrew, her husband, had faithfully committed to quietly raising this daughter as his own. Within several years of Taiye giving me the information about "a secret" within that family (Meredith's siblings had not known either), information which I never really paid much attention to, the Lord had let me know that the knowledge Taiye revealed to me represented an absolute *truthful fact*. It was not a fabrication of her own mind! While I had developed great respect for Taiye, because of her faith, integrity, and character, this confirmation that she was a person that the Lord was using in my life to establish my confidence in the reality of divine revelation and prophecy, according to His will, stunned me. I began to understand, know and accept that she been given the gift of prophecy. She was one to whom a truth had been spiritually revealed, and then passed on to me. God had used her as a messenger. It beget within me, in my inner being, a new hopeful way for me to seriously contemplate that dream she'd felt so strongly about sharing with me! *The one given to Taiye foretelling that my son "was going to be alright?"* The one where he was lifted up and saved within a church? If the one thing that had been spiritually revealed to her was *true*, and it *was*-then, what was I to think about the *other? Was that going to prove to be true also?*

Did I dare to hope for this and yes, even to expect it with steadfast persevering confidence?

Little did I know at the time what was to come some years later, regarding the prophetic dream concerning my son, who had continued thus far to be a captive of inherent sin, and to drown in the pit of the hell of alcoholism.

❁ ❁ ❁

"Follow the way of love and eagerly desire spiritual gifts, especially prophecy."

1 Corinthians 14:1 (NIV)

"But the one who prophesies speaks to people for their strengthening, encouraging, and consolation."

1 Corinthians 14:3 (NET)

Then he said to me "Prophesy to the breath; prophesy, son of man, and say to it, "This is what the sovereign Lord says: Come from the four winds, O breath, and breathe into these slain, that they may live."

Ezekiel 37:9 (NIV)

CHAPTER EIGHT

"Very rarely will anyone die for a righteous man, though
for a good man someone might possibly dare to die. But
God demonstrates his own love for us in this: While we
were still sinners, Christ died for us."

Romans 5:7-8 NIV

✞ *It is Mother's Day, May of 2006.* The driving rain is coming
down in torrents, and the roads are flooding, making many
highways impassable. It's the worst rainstorm I have ever witnessed
in my 53 years.

This past year has been just awful, horrible and discouraging in a
multitude of ways. 2005 was the year (previously mentioned) that I
had purchased a condo with and lived with my son and his pregnant
girlfriend who gave birth during that time. These living circumstances
provided me with a chance to be a close eye witness to how
entrenched Jared's existence had become in bondage to alcohol.

At this time, on this Mother's Day, the condo I'd purchased with
Jared is in the process of going into foreclosure, because the mortgage
unsurprisingly has not been paid since I wrenched myself away from
the unhealthy and enabling situation I'd found myself in. The mom
of my grandchild tried to stick it out for a few more months, doing
all she could, but then she had been left no choice but to flee back to
her mother's home for her own protection and welfare. My son
continues to live at the condo, mostly in drunkenness, and he seems

to be planning to do so until he is removed. It is a sorry situation. My heart is crushed with the disastrous way things have turned out, and by the accelerating slippery slope of alcoholism and destruction that Jared seems to be sliding down.

The rainstorm going on outside is torrential. I have asked my son earlier in the week, if, as his Mother's Day gift to me, he would accompany me to my church that I still attend regularly at Calvary Chapel Boston, in Rockland. My heart's desire is that he will get to hear the preaching of Pastor Randy Cahill while there, since Randy was such a powerful tool in the hands of the Lord used in my own life, for my salvation. I yearn for Jared to hear this Godly man preach. I also simply desire his company on this day, because despite everything that has unfolded and the many wrong and harmful things he has done, I still relish the company of this son of mine. Love covers a multitude of sins. (1 Peter 4:8) This is true of a father's love, a mother's love, and especially of our Father in heaven's love for His kids.

The powers of hell seem to join together to prevent Jared from keeping his promise to come along to church with me. First of all, there is the weather. All traveling advisories are telling people to forego their travel, as so many roads are flooding, or already severely flooded. When I arrive to pick him up at the agreed upon time, I find that he is unconscious in bed, and the room reeks of alcohol. For a moment I'm ready to give up, cave into self pity, and drown in my severe disappointment. Then the Holy Spirit speaks to my heart, and tells me to awaken him and remind him about going to church. The Spirit within reminds me not to be angry, to show only compassion and hopeful expectation that he'll keep his promise as I wake him. The Holy Spirit equips me with the self control that I completely lack in the natural.

I shake his shoulder gently-then harder. "Jared, I'm here to pick you up for church!" I sung out as if there was absolutely nothing "off" or askew about these circumstances. I said it in a tone as if I was my mom during my childhood, when she used to come into my sister's and my room and call out in a happy voice "Rise and shine!"

Jared went from being comatose to somewhat awake. "You'll have to hurry to take a shower so we can make it!" It may be hard for some to comprehend the next thing I will tell you. There has always been a form of integrity, often dormant within my Jared, yet there. From time to time it would reveal itself in his loyalty to keeping promises made to others that he loves, even when it was very hard for him. Please do understand that this occurred in the midst of many broken ones, as I have no desire to put a shiny polish on his sin or my own. As periodically and often regularly all of our character flaws will rear their ugly heads in our lives, in this case, it was a reversal of that fact. From time to time, amid much dominion of iniquity, this good quality in my son's character would rear it's noble head! Not steadfastly, not consistently, often dormant, but it was *in there*- a yearning evidenced by subsequent action to make good on a promise he'd made. As his mother I had occasionally seen it. This was one of those times. That characteristic ruled now, as he stumbled out of bed and into the shower. I was grateful.

The ride down to Rockland on the South Shore from Salem was ridiculously difficult. The visibility was next to nothing, as the rain poured down in river- like sheaths despite my wipers, down my windshield. It was relentless! The water level was sometimes up to the body of the car. By the grace and intention and purpose of the Lord, we made it to the church.

Ironically, the Lord had different plans on this day that I did. That often describes most of our walk with the Lord, does it not? My own plans were for Jared to hear Pastor Randy, whom I loved so much. The Lord's plans were for him to hear the testimony of the *visiting* Pastor that day, Poncho Juarez, a former addict, formerly dead in his sins, *except* that the Lord reached down to save him. Save Poncho He did! Poncho gave his powerful testimony on that very day to the congregation as Jared and I listened. It was clearly a divine appointment orchestrated by the Almighty for my son to hear...*while still reeking of alcohol and while spiritually dead.* (Romans 5:8-10) A "sort of" altar call was given at the end of the service, one in which instead of walking up to the front of the church to profess belief in Jesus, the usual venue- sinners who now chose to accept Christ publicly, were asked by Poncho to stand.

Jared stood. You could smell the booze from ten feet away, and he was cognizant of that, but he stood. In later years he confessed to me that he stood only to please *me* on that day. He said he wouldn't have responded to the call if he had had to walk up to the front of the church, because he was embarrassed that he reeked so badly. Do you believe the Lord can work with that? Does it touch the Lord's heart when a son, for a moment, puts aside his embarrassment and sense of false dignity and honors his mother?

For the next seven years, there was no evident sign of transformation.

I couldn't believe we made it home that day without obstacles- at some point Route One in Saugus became impassable due to severe flooding, and was closed to traffic. It was all over the evening news. That had never happened before, in the history of my life. It was as if the forces of hell had coordinated the timing to block us from reaching that church on that day. They did not obstruct the will of the Overcomer, yours and mine.

> "For at just the right time, while we were still powerless,
> the Messiah died for the ungodly."
>
> Romans 5:6, (NIV)

CHAPTER NINE

"But do not forget this one thing, dear friends: With the
Lord a day is like a thousand years, and a thousand
years are like a day. The Lord is not slow in keeping his
promise, as some understand slowness. He is patient
with you, not wanting anyone to perish, but everyone
to come to repentance."

2 Peter 3:8-9 (NIV)

"For a thousand years in your sight are like a day that has
just gone by"

Psalm 90:4 (NIV)

✝ *IT SEEMINGLY, FROM MY EARTHLY-SIGHT VIEW,* starts with a phone
call placed to me in January of 2013. Yet to be honest, I am
absolutely certain that it actually was signed and sealed by the hand
of the Almighty before the foundation of time. The salvation of any
one of us has been established for eternity. God's word makes that
clear. (Romans 8:29; Ephesian 1:4) I speak of the salvation of this
child of mine who was once a hopeless captive of sin, the sin that
we are *all* born into, this sinner child of my sinning flesh, whom I
love. I speak of his name, Jared, written on the palm of the Lord as
His very own, since before the beginning of time. Do not mock God
by scoffing at this dear one, for don't you know it is the gospel? All
are saved by faith alone.

I'm in my kitchen in Gloucester, MA on this extremely cold and wintry morning. I'm now married to Curt. It's very early in the new year. I answer the phone, and it's my son Jared calling from NYC. He has burned many bridges over the years. Been in and out of jail. Those familiar with this infirmity, this iniquity of the flesh named alcoholism, know the drill. He has been living in NYC with "friends" for about four years or so. No living situation he has ever been in has worked out. There have been *many.* They have all ended disastrously, due to his alcoholism and chronically bad choices. This is his sin playing out in his flesh and leading him to death. Physical death of course, but ever so awfully more alarmingly, spiritual death, which is eternal.

This week yet another brief living situation with some young woman has ended badly, and he has been kicked out. He's been on the streets for several days, I'm not sure exactly how long. It's bitterly cold outside, in the single digits. He's trying to survive by hanging out in various lobbies or waiting rooms until he is told to leave.

He asks me if I will give him money so that he can "come home." By this year the Lord has taught me through using my AL ANON attendance, and lots of painful experiences in which I made the wrong enabling sort of choices, that the "help" that we extend to the active alcoholics (or addicts) that we love is truly not any help at all, and it backfires, to *their and to our* detriment. This ultimately increases our own emotional suffering and agony beyond where it already is, and needlessly. It perpetuates a sense of hopelessness. It ruins our hearts, which we are instructed to guard. (Proverbs 4:23) To be blunt, the behavior of addicted loved ones will (Satan will use them to) suck the very heart and life out of us if we do not take a stand for the Lord's *ability alone.* It is alright, and yes, Godly, to guard one's own emotional health. This cessation of false helping and fixing ironically actually ultimately works *for* our addicted loved one's behalf. Our task is to climb out of our confusion over *whom* their Savior is. It is not us!

I accept and trust with all my mind, heart, soul and strength at this point in time, at long last, that my God is in control of both my life *and* Jared's. He is, and I *am not*. I believe fully that Jesus has completed the work and does not require my assistance to deliver my son from bondage. I need to live in accordance with believing all of that, with no "buts" or "if only I do such and such then…" attached. Living this way, in accordance to what the Lord has taught me through His word, makes me able to continue to be able to actively love my son deeply in my heart as his mom, while at the *same time* I compassionately refuse his request to give him money to "come home."I may have birthed him into the world physically, but it is only by a second spiritual birth that through Jesus Jared may receive the gift of spiritual life, which is the only true life in God's reality. When all in this life is said and done, being spiritually birthed is all that matters from the eternal perspective. (John 3:3-7)

There is a well known little book published by Al Anon Family Groups called "Courage to Change" that is well read thoughout the recovery community. When true and meaningful courage comes into our hearts and rules us, something we realize that we didn't possess within ourselves, it is always from the Lord, *never* from the self. That is why it is such an extraordinary quality! It's supernatural. Discovering that the courage has been provided, and taking the huge leap to act upon it, reflects the work of the Lord within you meant for your and for others' eternal behalf.

Again, the year of this phone call from NYC is 2013. I have been married since 2009 at this point in time to my husband Curt, a situation the Lord uses protectively in my behalf to make it a tiny bit easier for me to say "You can't live with me -what are your plans for a place to live if you came back?" To which my son responds "What do *you* think I should do mom?"

Oh, what a potential trap, a hook laden with bait. An invitation for me to play Savior. Get back Satan! I pray for the strength to not give into the temptation to provide my son with *my* answer, as the former version of me would have done prior to my new self. I now know now that it is *not I* on whom he needs to learn to rely. My carnal "self" as it's own entity is actually just as corrupted, useless and hopeless as my son's, and every other sinner's! So I say as gently and compassionately and congenially as I can "I don't know what you should do Jared, but I'm confident that you can figure it out, son. Let me know what you decide." This is fairly new behavior for me, that I have been learning and practicing in the past few years. When I hang up the phone moments later, I am praying fervently that there will be a break through for him. I am given a kind of peace and calm inside that does surpass all understanding (Phil 4:6.7), and am able to go on with my day instead of collapsing into a frantic state of despair and fear for him, a way I had often reacted many times in my past.

At some point over the next twenty four hours, the Holy Spirit brings it to my mind that there is some kind of a recovery house that has been started up by my church recently, for men with overriding, addictive, life disabling issues. I do not really know anything about it, so I call one of the young Pastor's wives, Amber Paik, who works faithfully at the church, to find out more. She kindly provides me with more information. After the conversation with her I am led, *led* being the key word, to make a decision to call my homeless son back, and make him an offer. This is completely Spirit directed! In other words, it is not my own idea, conceived from my own mind.

The Lord has brought me a long, long way in the past years teaching me how to detach from trying to micromanage my son's debilitating life issues. Only my growing, blooming faith has allowed me to make decision after decision to "LET GO and TRUST GOD." The Lord has made me into the mom who, through depending on the Lord's strength and being personally intimate with His mercy, can refuse to intervene in my son homelessness during deadly frigid weather. The mom who has repeatedly been able to, through faith in who Jesus is alone, ignore his phone calls from jail. Who has refused to buy him food via credit card over the phone when he is hungry, but has not worked. I am stunned at the changes in my behavior that stem from my trust in Him. Is that a boast? Absolutely! It is a boast in the power our Lord Jesus! I am learning about who Christ is, and beginning to experience the power of His resurrection-*because none of those behaviors reflect what I am in the natural, or what I am equipped to do in my own strength.* I am confident that as long as I haven't misheard the Holy Spirit, and that my perceived obedience is consistent with the Lord's directive timing, that my peace will not depart from me. It does not.

It is pretty simple. The Lord has prompted me by saying "Call and tell Jared you will pay for a bus ride back to MA (Boston) *on the condition* that he will speak with the Pastor (Mat Nadworny) at your church." That's it. That is what I feel the Lord has directed me to do: pay fifteen dollars for Jared to commute from New York to Boston on the Chinatown bus, with that one condition attached. He must agree to have a conversation with my pastor. I am clear on it that the Lord wills to use *me in order to* get him to the church, and then I am to detach from orchestrating any outcomes outside of His specific direction, and to leave it in His *Holy able hands.* No matter what happens. I call my son and extend the terms, and he agrees. The Lord has prepared both he and I for this time about to imminently unfold. Just as he has prepared you for whatever He is about to do next, in the activity your life, dearest reader.

It is also clear to me that the Lord had Jared in an extremely desperate crisis as a consequence of many years of tragic addictive behaviors spewing out of his genetics, and also was *providing* painful consequences in response to his choices around what to *do* with that flawed DNA. How I praise the Lord for that! We can not always recognize the blessings of the day. Who am I to judge Jared? At that time he was not a believer, not in the church.

I urge you to read the lyrics of Laura Story's song called "Blessings." The lyrics ask God if the rain, storms, and hardest times in our lives are His "mercies in disguise." God wants us to *recognize* His severe blessings and mercies dear one! They often come and arrive in radical disguise, as our Lord did after his death on the cross, to the two disciples walking on the road. *WHO ARE WE to judge and condemn any other?* Lousy, sin riddled DNA riddled with a huge propensity for alcoholism, combined with an upbringing of being raised by an ambitious agnostic worldly mother, were obvious factors contributing to and underlying my son's struggling in the deepest of pits. Or, maybe, do you think we might contemplate saying that "perhaps this has happened so that the glory of the one true God can be revealed?" Do you think we can say that about the ugly past histories of the lives of some Christ followers? About those of us that one day, at an appointed time in our lives, finally respond to His call? Believer, do you accept that our Lord can and will use a myriad of evil things to engineer the salvation of one of his chosen? *How big is your God? Is He bigger than every sin you have ever committed? Is He greater than your heart? Than every mess you have ever been in? Is He able to use all of it for your good?*

Is He able?

On Monday, January 7th, 2013 I drive into Brookline (greater Boston) to work, and shortly after 7 a.m. I leave my workplace for a few minutes to drive a mile up the street and pick up my son at the commuter rail. He looks in rough shape as he comes off the train, unshaven and unclean, and when he gets into the car he reeks of alcohol. We return to my workplace and he spends the majority of the day waiting inside my car in the parking garage, sleeping. I bring him some food at lunchtime. Much later in the afternoon, when the allergy practice is quieter and no patients are left, he comes in and waits in our department. My manager Dot very graciously says he is welcome to use a shower at another location in the building before we leave, and he takes her up on the kind offer.

I don't recall much about leaving work that night, or the ride back up Route 128 to the North Shore to Calvary Chapel, now renamed "Great Rock", in Danvers, MA. The Lord's *perfect* timing was evident to me when I realized that He had engineered that Jared would arrive at the church on a Monday night, the very night of the week they offer their "Broken Chains" ministry which begins at 7 p.m. It is a "Christian alternatives to addiction" group program which invites community members, believers and non, to come and be helped, encouraged and supported by one another in sober living. It's based on growing in faith, and trusting in and clinging to our all powerful and merciful God in order to walk soberly, free from any addiction.

What I do recall vividly, is turning into the parking lot of the church, off of Route 114. It was dark outside. I swung the car around, stopped near the entrance and said "Well here we are- Pastor Mat is in there." I nodded towards the door. Pastor Mat had been agreeable to speaking with Jared, of course.

Without further ado Jared got out of the car and headed into the church. I said "I love you" as he got out and walked away, and that was it. I drove home. I knew my part was finished. Jared had kept his part of the bargain.

I will always remember that visual of his walking away from the car in the winter darkness. I saw him through the eyes of Jesus. He'd been so vulnerable to the wiles of Satan while he'd been living out of his sin nature, just as I had in my own past. I watched him stride away, backpack strapped on his back, walking towards the doors of that church.

❁   ❁   ❁

The following morning, after being allowed to sleep in an empty trailer in the parking lot of the church all night, Pastor Mat and one or two other pastors from the church went and spoke with him. It is none of my business what transpired at that meeting, but during it I know that Jared committed to a year of living at "The Men of Valor in Training" program which is a faith based, bible teaching work program run by the church. It is a ministry for lost men who seek to take another road other than the destructive one they have been on. It became the first year of his adult life that he lived soberly. He also chose baptism. What a day of rejoicing that was! His stepfather Tim from whom I was divorced but still friendly, my mother, and I watched the story of this true conversion unfold with wonder, as he went down under the water.

"Lifted up on the arms of people from a church." Taiye's dream that she described to me! I was seeing it begin to unfold!

It is very incredible to me that seven years prior, at Calvary Chapel Boston where Randy Cahill serves as senior pastor, Jared had accompanied me to church on Mother's Day. He had stood at the call to stand "if you believe and accept Jesus *is* your Savior", and I quote Jared, "I stood to please *you* mom." Jared was trying to suggest to me, years later, that he was prompted internally to stand "for the wrong reason". I think not. He had a heart to honor his mother. The Lord saw. It pleased the Lord. God's ways *are mysterious* and who are we to say that *anything in the life of a believer happens in a wrong order?*

Do not despair loved ones. The Lord does not tarry and everything, ALL things, unfold according to His purpose.

May I encourage you to keep on praying relentlessly and yes, on your face for those the Lord has brought into your life, no matter what circumstances look like on the surface? Put your confidence into standing on the promises of our Lord. Do not get weary of waiting and give up. Renew yourself daily by reading and studying God's word, and pray to Him, in order to be refilled and replenished with the strength and hope and supernatural patience of the indwelling Spirit!

This particular salvation story of my son's transformation, of his being made a *new creature in Christ,* did not end there. None of our transformation stories end after initial salvation when it is real! Our stories are just starting to get really, *really interesting! Growing in Christ, coming to maturity is what awaits the reborn infant Christian!*

"...just as he chose us in the Messiah before the creation of the universe to be holy and blameless in his presence. In love he predestined us for adoption to himself through Jesus the Messiah, according to the pleasure of his will, so that we would praise his glorious grace that he gave us in the Beloved One."

Ephesians 1:5,6 (ISV)

As he went along, he saw a man blind from birth, "Rabbi, who sinned, this man or his parents, that he was born blind?"

"Neither this man or his parents sinned,"said Jesus, but this happened so that the works of God might be displayed in his life."

John 9:1-3 (NIV)

CHAPTER TEN

"So I find this law at work: When I want to do good, evil is right there with me. For in my inner being I delight in God's law: but I see another law at work in the members of my body, waging war against the law of my mind and making me a prisoner of the law of sin at work within my members. What a wretched man am I! Who will rescue me from this body of death? Thanks be to God-through Jesus Christ our Lord!"

Romans 7:21-25 (NIV)

✠ THE YEAR IS 2017. I have been seeking and following Christ since approximately the year 2000. I am now a full on for Christ believer. I am captivated by a deep thirst and yearning to know more of God's truth. In my mind, I hunger to be a slave for Christ's sake, a suffering servant, to be His trophy, to be continuously sanctified for His name's sake. I still stumble, albeit less than before. He always picks me up and renews me. I am becoming ever more keenly, intensely aware not just of my own specific sins, but of my ever present sin nature, sin always living in me and pressing to dominate. It's a two fold issue. Yet, I am so encouraged despite the pressing battle, to simultaneously have radical changes in who I am and how I operate in this foreign world continuously revealed to me, as the years of my life go by. All God's hand. I cling, often desperately, to God's mercy as I know without Christ I have *no righteousness.*

HE is my only righteousness.

The spiritual warfare is ongoing. My understanding is that it will remain that way while in this body. My propensity to fall, to backslide into what I am in the natural, is ever present. My sin feels like "sticky fly paper" that I just can't get off of me! I can still slide into being prideful, judgmental, critical, ruled by vanity, and competitive. I'm still aware of the inner lurking ungodly temptation to exhibit myself as better than others, of often being downtrodden by guilt (a sin!), and of believing the lie that heaven, for me, will be a result of my own works (Gal. 2:21).

This year I am attending the Calvary Chapel East Coast Pastors' Wives Conference in the town of Northeast, Maryland. It is late April. I'm serving as a hostess. How I love that I "get to" to do this! This is an annual retreat for Calvary Chapel pastors' wives designed to teach, refresh, encourage, counsel, renew and restore them. A group of Christian sisters from Calvary Chapel in Rockland serve there yearly, and I have been included in the invitation to do so for several years. What a blessing it is for me! It is the church where I was first saved, where I walked up to the front to make a public profession of my decision to follow Christ and express the belief that He and He alone by grace is my Savior; the only means by which I can be reconciled to God. This group serving at the conference includes my biological sister Diane, which adds another layer of sweetness to the trip. Our role as hostesses is small, and includes duties like greeting and directing, passing things out, and setting up and tidying rooms. The rewards are incomparably great! Getting to listen to all the teachings and to worship and fellowship with all these dear ladies with a heart for God is *rich*. I treasure my time with them. When I am there, there has been nowhere else in the world I would prefer to be. Nowhere.

While wintering on Amelia Island Florida during the earlier

months of 2017, and former years as well, I have been studying God's word with an anointed Christian teacher by the name of Jan Smith, who operates out of the multi denominational Chapel located at "The Plantation". She and her husband Barney run many bible classes. It's the community where my husband Curt and I reside to escape the harshness of New England's winters. In one of the studies that God has put on Jan's heart to teach, she uses (as a springboard to get us into the truth of the word) a book written by Watchman Nee called "The Normal Christian Life." Her personal story of the Lord leading her to this book many years ago, reveals His indisputable activity in her Christian walk. She has been a willing instrument in the hands of the Lord through effective teaching of Nee's book as she shares how the Lord changed her own understandings and grew her in knowledge and wisdom, using its contents, all of which are deeply rooted in God's word. Her eagerness to share what she has learned is strong and bold and marked by astounding perseverance. Those yearning to grow in Christian maturity seek out her classes and the Lord brings them in when He has them ready. My life, my real life in and through Jesus that is, has been drastically enriched and deepened by what I have been learning there through studying God's word over several years now, while partaking in this study during my winter months. This is the place and setting in which the Lord has worked through Jan to instruct me in the meaning of "walking in the spirit." It is perfectly summed up in Galatians 2:20:

"I have been crucified with Christ, and I no longer live, but Christ lives in me. The life I live in the body I live by faith in the Son of God, who loved me and gave himself for me." (NIV)

When God has brought me to the place where I understand that whatever is born of my flesh (my self *apart* from Jesus) has zero eternal spiritual value, and that life will be *given* as I die again and again to the reign of my natural self, as I trust that the Holy Spirit is sealed in me, my life *becomes* holy and pleasing to the Father. This willing and conscious exchange of my carnal self for the reign of His holy life within me, springs from faith. The self- type thinking, that is, the believing that we have something worthy to offer to the Father that springs from the natural man, dies a hard and reluctant death. Satan our tempter is bent on keeping the self directed person thriving and unconscious of their need for God's love and provision, and thus on keeping us separate from God.

During this particular season, as no other, the Holy Spirit has kept this verse, Galatians 2:20, in the forefront of my mind and I have pondered and meditated on it continuously. I have repeated it to myself intermittently throughout the day, every day, for many months.

It is the last session of the final full day at the pastor's wives' conference, and I am feeling enriched, satisfied, joyful and content in my spirit. As usual, it has been a fruitful conference. I am at peace, that is, until the final activity of the last full day is announced. I believe it was Pastor Randy Cahill's wife Cheryl who announced to the three hundred plus ladies in the room what we were going to do next. It rattled me greatly! I was immediately on guard and even contemplated leaving the room!

The directive went something like this- "Ladies, we are going to darken the room, and ask all the women to close their eyes and bow their heads and pray. If the Holy Spirit brings to your mind a scripture verse that you believe in your heart is a word for someone else, please announce it out loud."

I was mortified! As I immediately defaulted into "leaning on my own understanding" instead of leaning into my faith, I speculated in my mind that we were all in immediate danger of inviting the activity of Satan himself into the room. Was it not fully possible, I reasoned, that perhaps one of the more "immature in Christ" ladies present might succumb to the temptation to try to showcase *herself*? That, in a weaker moment, driven by pride and our ever lurking opportunistic lust for self glory (I confess I recognize it because it's exactly what I can be), some weaker sisters may act directly out of their flesh and in doing so, dabble in the realm of a form of sorcery? Stumble into the temptation of seeking attention as if they, *from their own nature* had the power, ability, and knowledge to communicate what only God knows, to another? Would not *only our Lord* (Holy Spirit) know what scripture verses someone else needed to hear?

Little did I realize that every one of my thoughts in those very moments failed miserably to spring from faith.

As I toyed with the idea of walking out of the large room, because I knew I didn't want to knowingly be part of any activity that may tempt another to stumble, and while listening with my head bowed down as directed, a voice rang out:

"I don't know who this scripture is for, but someone out there needs to hear GALATIANS 2:20."

Oh, what a wonderful moment. Note to self-a believer in the room, through the power of the Spirit of Christ our Lord, was filled with the knowledge of exactly what one of her sisters needed to hear. The power came from Jesus and He worked through her. She spoke out in obedience, driven by her faith and the Spirit within, to do so. Had I doubted that the Holy Spirit was there moving in that room with us? Oh ye of little faith. Forgive me Lord!

> "And immediately Jesus stretched forth his hand, and caught him, and said unto him, O thou of little faith, wherefore didst thou doubt?"
>
> Matthew 14:31 (KJV)

CHAPTER ELEVEN

"Be reconciled to God. God made him who had no sin to be sin for us, so that in him we might become the righteousness of God."

2nd Corinthians 5:21 (NIV)

"For he chose us in him before the creation of the world to be holy and blameless in his sight. In love he predestined us to be adopted as his sons through Jesus Christ, in accordance with his pleasure and will-to the praise of his glorious grace which he has freely given us in the One he loves."

Ephesians 1:4-6 (NIV)

✠ I laugh with joyful laughter and glee now in the present fall season of 2019 when I recall what a wretched mess my life was in the years before Jesus imparted His life into me. Let the reader not misinterpret what I write. He came in so many clear ways to me, not to really *improve my life* I was living in the flesh, because spiritually I was dead, and did not require an improvement on that hopeless version for salvation. That is God's perspective, friend, which we find in our Bibles.

How can there be an uplifted version of "DEAD in our sins"? He sought me for His purpose of imparting to me His life. He came and comes still, to teach me through His word, through His Spirit, through divinely engineered experiences, and through spiritually equipped beloved teachers in multiple forms, to lay my own life down, in exchange for His. I laugh not so much because of my former sin not being counted against me by the Father, which is cause for great celebration, but because I recognize the profound differences in *myself and in how I live, and think, and desire and deem things as important or unimportant.* The extreme, radical internal change in how I operate while in this flesh stems from His grace alone. He has put a treasure within this earthen vessel made of dust, and it replaces everything I have ever counted as having value. He alone has done it. He has engineered the astounding exchange of my life for His. Prior to being saved, which the word tells me was always the glorious plan that the Lord had for me, I was literally a dead woman walking, as all those are that that have rejected Christ and who persist in that stance.

It's not that I am now free from having to reckon with the constant presence of the Adamic nature within me, which seeks relentlessly to dominate my fleshly life while I am in this body. It is that I *know that I am weak and have a Savior that is strong. It is that I reckon my flesh as dead, without hope. Christ has done and will continue to do the work, and I don't have to. That's the joy! It's holy joy!* The pressure is completely off of me to work my way to an eternity with our Father through perfect law keeping and by my own good works. Christ himself has convicted me through knowledge of his word, enmeshed intimately with personal experience He has provided, that the law is beyond all of our collective abilities to keep it. The command to trust and walk with Jesus, knowing it is He who has fulfilled the law in my behalf, rules my heart and activity- although like a child, I often forget to let it be so. What a relief that I can lean on him in every moment as I choose by the power of the Spirit, to set my own self aside and let Him lead. Any works He accomplishes through me *will* be counted (hallelujah!) because they represent the fruit that comes from *my dying,* and *His power and ability.* It will be *His* work.

Living this way is an inevitable trigger for intensified spiritual warfare as Satan schemes more viciously to make me fall, to weaken my faith and my confidence in Jesus's work. Fear of that is mitigated as I recall it is Jesus Himself that has set my feet firmly on the rock and through Him (only) I stand! It is He who set me free from the law of sin and death, by the law of the Spirit of life that comes through Christ Jesus.

I now know that I can be one of two creatures in any moment of life. One choice is to let who I am in the natural rule over me (my own mind, will and emotions) and lead me in the way of spiritual death, or at least keep me stuck without growth as a carnal infant Christian; or, I may choose to accept that if I claim the promise, and am *born again by the Spirit,* I can *exchange my life* for the power of Jesus's life, which will work through me. I must constantly be willing to die to my own flesh, often moment by moment. It's ongoing choice while here. Only through His grace and power do we, can we, persevere in doing so.

I am *free* because that wicked wretched evil heart within has been conquered for all time and for all peoples. It's a done deal. God's people are sealed with his Spirit, the guarantee of our inheritance until redemption.(Ephesians 1:13-14) This is God's promise to us! It's for Jew and gentile believers alike. How wonderful! The victory that our Lord won in our behalf, that He paid the price to secure and then to make available to me after He has made me His, sets me free. He has *and will continue to* justify me in the eyes of the Father and this rests on nothing that I have done or will or can ever do, except *believe the truth* and *cling to Jesus. He will do all the rest of it, including any designated good work that will follow* that *will* be counted in heaven. It is He who accomplishes the changes in me. Always all Him.

> "For we know that our old self was crucified with him so that the body of sin might be done away with, that we should no longer be slaves to sin-because anyone who has died has been freed from sin."
>
> Romans 6:6-7 (NIV)

❀ ❀ ❀

The year is 2001. It becomes an evening riddled with and defined by unholy anger. I pray that any reader will be struck with observing a radical contrast between what I tell you I *now* am, with and by the indwelling Spirit, and the self centered woman in this chapter. I insist that in the present it is true that I been born anew from what I once was. I acknowledge that without doubt I have the potential to lapse back into that old person, and behave as she at any moment, unless it is He who carries me forward. I have found He is faithful and does so.

I am leaving work, my nursing position after working ten and a half hours in Brookline one night. Instead of heading north to drive home to the North Shore as I usually do, my plan is to drive to the Marriot in Quincy to attend the Calvary Chapel women's annual retreat. It's the first weekend in November. I will meet my sister Diane there. I'm single for seven years at this time, having been divorced *twice*.

Physically I am exhausted, having been up since 4:30 a.m. I'm a bit miffed with my sister, that instead of making a plan to meet me for dinner, she has volunteered to assist with registration! I am thus going to be on my own until the worship and speakers get started at 7:30 p.m. Doesn't she value spending time with ME? I was completely at the center of my world.

Shortly after starting to drive, I call my running partner and friend Kitty and we begin to do the female "gab." We are discussing life pressing issues like where we get our nails done and supplements that will preserve our health and beauty, and *other people* (a favorite topic) It was the same old. It starts to lightly snow, and Route 128 is becoming a little slippery. The weather is cause in my mind to become even more cranky, and I feel quite entitled to feeling that way. Poor me!

I suddenly realize that I have slipped into "automatic" behavior and I am driving *north* on Route 128, towards my home, as I mindlessly chatter away. The retreat is in Quincy, towards the South Shore. The traffic is heavy, the roads are getting increasingly slippery, and I have just wasted 20 minutes headed in the wrong direction! With another 20 minutes to recover my ground, it will be a waste of at least forty minutes of slippery dangerous travel, to get back to where I started from!

My mood worsens, and my self pity increases. After a trying long day at work, I feel as if I am going to "blow a gasket."Self pity reigns! I may have used some foul language. Actually, ignore my attempt at cleaning up the confession, I did for sure.

The driving becomes treacherous, and I finally make it to the Quincy Marriot and park in the back lot. I remove my stiff white knuckled hands from wheel, get out of the car and then trudge through the snow which is still coming down heavily, dragging my suitcase behind me. I make it inside. I'm feeling at the "end of my rope" and simply can not cope with one more thing not going *my* way or in *my* favor. I just want to whine and have someone understand how horribly I have perceived my day to have unfolded! I get it in my head that nothing can soothe me except tossing down my favorite social drink, to chemically "take the edge off", which is a lemon drop martini.

There's sis...*helping with registration. Hrrumph!* As usual, she's putting the ladies at church before respecting her older *sister* and cherishing the rare amount of time she gets to spend with me. I'd never treat her with such carelessness! I'm fuming now. I grab the room keys and head up to our room.

I'm extremely startled when I open the door to what I think will be an empty room and there stands- a *stranger!* How could this be happening? They must have given me the wrong room key.

"Hi I'm Kathy" says this person. "You must be Diane's sister-I'm sleeping in your room with you and Diane." I am horrified. Seriously? I need peace and quiet and have no desire to share a bathroom with not *one* but *two* ladies. Only because my parents taught me good manners, and because I am not by nature unkind, am I able to restrain myself from angrily expressing my dismay. I have heard about Diane's good friend Kathy for several years now, but I have *no desire to know her* and even less than that to share sleeping and dressing space with her. My frustration and indignation with my sister Diane is multiplied! I can't believe she didn't inform me about this! I can't recall the last time I was so "ticked off."

Now I have to eat dinner with this stranger lady! "Oh brother", I think, now I'm going to be expected to make polite conversation *and I don't want to. I am completely done and running on empty."* Truly, what I wanted was to wallow in self pity and the multiple tragedies of my tiring stressful day, while gulping down a martini to drug away my self justified mood. Yes, this was me, the so called (new) Christian woman (not) at the end of my work week, attending a Christian women's retreat.

As I resentfully sat at dinner with Kathy to my left, I continued to simmer with negativity. I don't recall what we talked about but I do recall how quickly I drained that martini while it fluttered through my mind briefly "I wonder what this goody two shoes thinks of this! She just has no idea how stressed I am! She's probably never had a martini in her life!"

And thus that was how the second Christian retreat I'd ever gone to with my sister Diane began.

❋　❋　❋

"When you were slaves to sin, you were free from the control of righteousness. What benefit did you reap at that time from the things you are now ashamed of? Those things result in death. But now that you have been set free from sin and have become slaves to God, the benefit you reap leads to holiness, and the result is eternal life. For the wages of sin is death, but the gift of God is eternal life in Christ Jesus our Lord."

Romans 6:20-23 (NIV)

Fifteen years later, and I am in a bedroom at a retreat in Maryland with Diane and Kathy and a handful of other women who have affirmatively answered the precious invitation to serve at the Calvary Chapel East Coast Pastor's Wife's Conference. It's bedtime, and I lie in a bed beside my dear, sweet precious sister in Christ, Kathy. Diane has often shared a bed with Kathy in past years when we do things together, often with multiple women in a room, but Diane needs a bed to herself this year because of back problems, so she takes the twin bed. I happily volunteer to share the one queen bed with Kathy. There is another Christian sister in the other twin bed, Judy.

As the four of us are getting more cozy as we settle into the mattresses beneath us, Kathy begins to pray out loud. She presents multiple petitions to our Lord with praise and thanksgiving. I think of what a privilege it is to be sharing my sleeping space with such a dear and faithful daughter of the Lord beside me. A peace and sense of divine safety settle over me, as I never knew in my former life. I fall into a grateful, sweet sleep while chuckling in my mind and wondering what the former version of me would have thought of this scene. How mortified and shocked that old woman would have been at what the new woman considered to be her treasure.

❖ ❖ ❖

"So then, if anyone is in Christ, he is a new creation; what is old has passed away-look, what is *new* has come!"

2nd Corinthians 5:17 (NIV)

"...join with me in suffering for the gospel, by the power of God, who has saved us and called us to a holy life-not because of anything we have done but because of his own purpose and grace."

2 Timothy 1:8-9 (NIV)

CHAPTER TWELVE

"For the Lord disciplines those he loves; just as a father disciplines the son in whom he delights."

Proverbs 3:12 (NET)

✠ *I BELIEVE THE LORD WOULD HAVE ME SPARE* most of the details of the following sad, embarrassing, but encouraging story, so I will make it shorter than most. It has to do with some "adjustment strains, struggles and growing pains" that occurred during one of the early years of what is my third marriage, to my dear husband Curt. So these events probably occurred in 2010 or 2011.

As many people who enter into marriages late in life have experienced, it is not really common for things to go smoothly, that is, without significant issues and conflicts especially when attempting to cultivate working relationships with each other's grown adult children. Territorial and temporal issues present themselves when a new wife moves into a long established home of her new husband, and there are inevitably sad and trying conflicts of interest as the landscape of familiar family culture inevitably drastically changes. Sin natures of all involved get provoked, and often percolate, and change is resisted. It's often hard, and challenging for all involved. Let's all remember these types of circumstances were never part of God's original perfect plan for us, His design, or His first desire for His kids. (theologians may debate this point, because perhaps we may consider the possibility that it *was.* God has not revealed *all* to us in His word, only that which He would have us know *now*)

One night in March, I found myself out with my husband and his two grown children who were in their forties, their partners, and a lovely aunt of theirs, at a notorious sort of hard core Gloucester bar, "The Rhumb Line". The group had agreed (and I went passively along with it to avoid upsetting my husband) to reconvene there, after a family group birthday dinner, for "one more drink."

Now, I was seething internally at what *I* had, in my own mind, construed as significant rudeness and disrespect that had occurred at my home earlier from one of the grown children, and their spouse. In retrospect it now seems quite silly, but I was very hurt by something that was most likely unintentional. "Getting through" this night had become a real challenge for me. I was smoldering with hurt and anger, and did not want to be there. I was convinced that I had been treated extremely disrespectfully by at least two adults that were present.

So what did I do? Let me confess to the reader first, what I completely failed to do. I did *not pray.* Yes, this is now about ten years into my walk with the Lord. I did *not* cry out to the Lord for His sovereign strength, to help me make it through the night, since I knew how weak and ill equipped I was to handle this situation gracefully in the natural. I did *not* ask Him to use me as a vessel of His love, grace and mercy. I thought *not* of forgiveness, "for they know not what they do." I thought not of remaining *still,* or finding peace during the storm going on in my heart, by *knowing he is God.* I defaulted into my sin nature, refusing to die to what I am in the natural, to all the inner turmoil that was festering, and so thus sin dominated. Self pity (again!) and self derived action took over. None of it was Spirit-led.

Here is what happened. Curt and I arrived first at the "seedy" place following dinner. I think his kids thought it was "funny", sort of "humorous" to all go there. I understand that, because I would have at one time, too. I sat at the bar beside my husband while we were waiting on the others to arrive, and I quickly ordered a strong drink and gulped it down like a drug to numb my internal indignant fury stemming from hurt feelings. I'm ashamed and humbled to write how many years this was into my Christian walk that this occurred. The way I sometimes (although quite rarely) resorted to gulping alcohol in a crisis might have you thinking I had a "problem" and yes I did, of the worst kind. It wasn't alcoholism though, it was still spiritual. It was a lack of *complete and total* trust in God to be present in every circumstance of my life, and to work it out for my eternal good. Great carnal Christian example I am while operating out of the flesh! What an opportunity lost. The memory is not a good one! It's quite horrible.

The drink hit me pretty hard, and I felt more than a "little woozy." A little while later, someone ordered another drink for me and my better judgment, long gone, once again did not prevail. Nor did the desire to keep my focus on behaving in a manner pleasing to the Lord ever even enter my mind. I had made the lethal ungodly decision that it was the sedating effects of alcohol that I was going to lean on for *this* night, and *not* the power of the Holy Spirit within me. Within moments of receiving the second drink into my hand, I dropped it (or was that God?) and it loudly shattered all over the place. I appeared like a drunken fool. I looked *nothing* like a daughter of the Most High.

Now, although I was never historically in my life a heavy social or even a regular drinker, and biologically was spared from suffering with a physical weakness for or continuous craving for alcohol, during my adult agnostic and even early Christian years I had partaken enough during "parties" and other social events to be all too familiar with what a "hangover" felt like. I have to confess and honestly admit to the reader that many times in my past, I had drank the equivalent, perhaps more, of what I partook of on *this* night! Yet never, ever, *ever* did I suffer so much or so long with the ill effects, as I did on the following day.

Curt and I eventually went home from the Rhumb Line on that awful embarrassing night, and I began to vomit sometime in the wee morning hours after "passing out" in our bed. That throwing up continued and continued, and continued. At two o'clock the following afternoon, I believe it was a Saturday, I was still vomiting and still lying in bed with an enormously painful headache. Others who had drank as much as I had and more the previous evening, had gone on with their weekend activities. Meanwhile, I suffered extremely from being so stupid and foolish-reaping what I sowed from my failure to run to the Lord for strength I did not have to endure my perceived insult and rejection. I could not understand why the ill effects were so much more intense, longer in duration, and drastically more debilitating than they had ever been in my past! It was so confusing to me, until the Lord spoke quietly again to me, in my mind, later in the afternoon as I remained suffering in bed.

"IT'S BECAUSE YOU ARE MINE, AND I LOVE YOU SO MUCH. *YOU ARE NOT TO DO THAT.*"

I suddenly *saw what He was doing,* and what amazing gratitude filled my heart! He was not going to let me get away with choosing what was so harmful to me, without harsh discipline. More importantly, He was not going to allow me to get away with claiming to be His own, while publicly behaving like a drunken imbecile. It ruined and *destroyed* my testimony.

I was never, ever, so grateful to receive discipline like this in my life. Years later, as I write this, I partake of alcohol rarely, and then only one drink. This is usually on the unique occasion that I am out on a special dinner or social event with my husband, whom I love. Even then, I choose to have one if *he* desires one, with the good heart motive of feeding a sense of camaraderie with something that for *me* is not a problem. God made our hearts, and He sees their motives. The *same* activity is made either sinful or acceptable in the eyes of God, according to a person's purpose in their heart.

Thus I am saying that I believe that our God looks at one's intentions or disposition in drinking alcohol, when they decide to partake. Think about the prayer activities of Jewish pharisees from Jesus's time being radically displeasing to God, when they prayed on street corners for purposes of showing off how "Godly" they were. Wrong motive, based on ungodly desire. (they were seeking self glorification) God hates that, when our motives do not align with His will. God distinguishes by looking at our hearts, so we must all search our own with candidness. If you have ever been in bondage to alcohol, if it has owned you, you *must avoid it* as diligently as John the Baptist did, unless you want to settle for a wasted, unfruitful life of pain and drunkenness, and worse.

For me personally, I have quietly declared it in my heart a sort of partial "fast" in which I dedicate either the abstinence or self control (in the form of "just one") to the Lord. Self control is fruit of the Spirit. God *will* provide the self control for us that we lack, if we ask. We often tend to make idols out of indulgence and pleasure, rather than just receiving and enjoying the blessings in the context of loving and depending on God. Our Father does enjoy giving His children gifts, and wants us to enjoy what He has provided, while realizing that we have nothing that He did not provide. It has been true for most of my life that in my flesh I do really enjoy a good social drink or even two, "just" from time to time. I had often abused that freedom socially in my earlier Christian life. "All things are lawful for me-but not everything is beneficial" is written in 1 Corinthians 6. It is tempting to attempt to clean up or neutralize our disobedience with scriptures like that one. The fact is, we are no longer under the law, albeit it is Holy. We are sinners under *grace*. Further on in the same chapter we are told "For you were bought at a price. Therefore glorify God with your body."

I must make it clear to you that I have not chosen to change my personal habits on drinking alcohol as a form of "penance", because that would indicate that I believe that it is my work *and not the blood of Christ* that atones for my sin. It would indicate that I ascribe to the idea of *works* of the self being necessary to *earn* one's salvation, not grace *alone*. I confess to my reader, it's a "little bit hard" sometimes for me to say "no thanks" in certain social scenarios, especially because in the flesh I am oriented by nature and nurture to "people pleasing". This characteristic is a sin when it pulls us away from the One who desires that we please Him only. It can and will obstruct the work He might do through us. Christians seriously walking with the Lord must be prepared for the world not to like them. There is often pressure from others to partake in many sorts of indulgences that are pleasurable for a short time, but outside of the way God asks us to live. We must all decide what is most important to us. In general, when many people drink, they really seem to like it a *whole lot* when others join in.

Indulgence and gluttony love company. We are all predisposed to choose and pursue pleasure seeking. We all can and often do lust for the carnal reward of that temporary flesh satisfaction in the moment. Have you ever noticed that? I find that when I want to do good, evil is always right there too. There's the battle! I sometimes do want to join in with the excess of overindulgence and get rewarded not only with lots of pleasure, but also by feeling like "one of the group". Yes, that's right, at 66 years old. Temptation remains.

I often cave in. Let it be, I tell myself. Christ has fixed it, let me ask Him to keep changing me.

It is a kingdom privilege to be outcast, and share in the sufferings of Christ, even so very lightly as with a bit of self denial, and a little bit of rejection from others who think we're weird, whilst our hearts are being purified, and surely none of this by our own efforts. It is happening all along, this sanctification process. It is happening because of and by the finished work of Christ when we are seeking to be pleasing to the Lord in any way, even the minutest ways.

All believers are Christ's trophies, and we are his holy works in progress. Do not mistake this dear reader, as I erroneously believing that changing any one of my personal habits makes me a "better" person. It does not! Without Christ there is no such thing as a "better person." This is God's perspective. Without Christ, and without the seal of the Holy Spirit, all of humanity is unacceptable to the Father due to our Adamic nature of sin. Some call this original sin. Don't make the natural human mistake of offering to our Lord a worthless penance! What He wants is for us to recognize, to *see our sin before we can be healed*, like when Moses lifted up the snake in the desert! Look at it! Only Christ justifies, and regarding that work, He now commands me to keep writing... "It is finished!" That which His work obtained in my behalf I may receive by grace. The Lord's perspective is radically different from our own understanding. A proud person can not see their sin.

There are only two groups- those in whom He sees His son (sheep); and those in whom He does not see His son (goats). There are children that He foreknew before the foundation of the world, and non-children. He has not known the goats. There is true Israel, and non-Israel. (Romans 11) Co-inheritors with Christ, and non-inheritors. Some of his sheep surely drink socially, and enjoy fabulous feasts, as did Jesus, without being one smidgeon displeasing to the Father. Remember, there is no condemnation for those that are in Christ Jesus. All believers have been set free from the law of sin and death. "Everything is permissible"-but not everything is "beneficial."Let's remember that, loved ones. "Love God, and do as you please", said Saint Augustine. Ask the Holy Spirit to show you what that means in *your* life, in *your* individual walk with the Lord. This holy walk is extremely personal, yes, our Lord is extremely personal in His relationship with *just you, whom He loves without measure.*

It is a challenge to smile sadly at this vile memory of my drunkenness in the presence of my husband's family on the night I've written about, rather than wallow in self disgust and shame, but I do sadly smile and shake my head at myself. Oh, we are so wretched without Him leading us, when we won't listen and apply. His yoke is easy and His burden light, my friend. I do not doubt His power to work powerfully within me to cleanse and transform. I do not doubt the power of the blood of Jesus, which is exactly why I can speak and write publicly of my own horrendous sin and vast shortcomings. He died to redeem me from the consequences of sin and it is truly wrong for any of his children to waste precious time, the brief vapor of their life on earth, wallowing in their guilt. Get up, get up Christian believer and keep going! The guilt that captivates and immobilizes a child of God suggests that this believer buys the lie that Christ's payment on their behalf may not have been sufficient. It *was sufficient!* We must not believe that we must add something to it. Let recognition of your sin and guilt lead you to confession and repentance, *that* is all that is required. Throw yourself at the foot of the finished work of the cross and allow His mercy to win you more deeply. How I thank you, Lord, for ensuring that I came to eventually know that all of this is true.

"Blessed is the man whom God corrects; so do not despise the discipline of the Almighty."

Job 5:17 (NIV)

"For He maketh sore, and bindeth up: He woundeth, and His hands make whole."

Job 5:18 (KJV)

CHAPTER THIRTEEN

"And my God will supply every need of yours according
to his glorious riches in Christ Jesus."

"New Morning Mercies"
devotional by Paul Tripp

✝ AFTER I RETIRED FROM NURSING at Brigham and Women's
Hospital in December of 2015, when I was sixty two, my
husband Curt (whom I married in 2009) and I decided that we
would start an "Airbnb" business in our home, the following
summer. The space in our above the ground basement area of our
home where the grandchildren used to hang out, play ping pong
and sleep when they were younger, was similar to a "mother in law"
apartment. It included a small kitchenette area, a bathroom, and had
its own entrance.

Since we live in Gloucester, MA, which is a wonderful summer
and fall destination for tourists to visit, our venture was enormously
successful. The Lord sent us really wonderful, respectful "guests"
and I discovered that I got much satisfaction from now being in the
field of hospitality! Many of the guests ended up sharing with me,
sometime during their stay with us, that they too were believers. I
think they were encouraged to do after they saw the nature of *some*
of the readings in the cozy "reading corner" I had set up which were
Christian. That was always a sweet blessing to me. I found out that
I was pretty gifted at the hospitality piece, and spent much time

trying to come up with new ideas of how I could help people feel more welcome. Curt would make gentle fun of me, telling others that I was greatly diluting our profits by spending them back on the renting guests that came.

One summer day when we were expecting paying guests to arrive, I was running way behind. There were some items that I needed to stock in the small guest refrigerator that I did not have in supply. I had barely enough time to hurry to the supermarket and purchase them, and then finish my preparations before the guests arrived. In addition to all the basic cleaning and disinfecting and food prep, my list of "to dos" also included taking a shower and being presentable to welcome the guests myself, along with Curt. I liked to have everything "just right" when our paying guests checked in. It was important to me.

I have always intensely disliked having to rush and hurry. It makes me nervous and cranky. I get irritated with myself, or with whatever circumstances lead me to my needing to rush. The result is a "bad mood." I recall being quite anxious and overwhelmed as I rushed over to Stop and Shop to grab the needed items. I feared that my guests would arrive early, and that I would not have the rental space in our home, our small in-law type apartment, all set up for them *exactly* the way I liked it to be. The way I behaved, you would have thought it was a matter of life and death.

I flew through the store gathering the items in my grocery cart. I'm sure I felt very impatient as I waited my turn for the cashier to check me out. Of course it seemed as if I was in the slowest line. Like a complete dope, and as if I were a Godless creature, I had worked myself into a frenzy of nerves. Have you ever stood with any unpleasant person like that in a line, devoid of patience-or been that person?

After the two or three minutes in line that seemed like thirty in my sorry mind, it was finally my turn to pay, and I could not find my credit card. I did not have it on me. I didn't have time for this delay! Then I recalled that I had set up "apple pay" on my i-phone earlier in the week, and so I tried to use that method to pay, even though I'd never yet used it. Neither I nor the cashier could get that to work. She called the manager over to assist. By this time my dismay must have been clearly evident. There was no way I could make it home and return with the payment, *and* be ready for my Airbnb guests too. I was about to fail completely in my endeavor. How I hate failing in standards I have set for myself! Truth be told however, I often have.

The customer behind me in the line said "Here dear, I'm just going to loan you the cash."

I remember turning to her, a slightly older woman, in stunned shock and replying with great surprise "But you don't even know me! Why would you do that?" She answered me "Because you have a trustworthy face." I was blown away to hear that she thought that, because in that moment of time I felt like a screaming banshee inside. There was nothing outwardly nice about me at all. I pridefully replied to her "I don't know you so thank you, but I can't take your money." I called my husband on the phone to see if he would check the balance in the account that I had attached the "Apple Pay" to, to ascertain that it had enough money in it. It did. It just wasn't going to work. With great frustration I apologized to the cashier and said I wouldn't be able to take my food items.

The woman behind me said "You could take them with you if you would just agree to let me loan you this money."

It came to me in a flash of understanding. "It is the Lord!" He was rescuing me in this moment, even though I was behaving like a total jerk- losing my peace over such silly things, failing to turn to Him, and pridefully dismissing the kind offer of assistance from a stranger that *He* had chosen to work through on this day. All that was required of me was to humble my haughty self and accept the offer of God to provide help through a kind stranger. She was a vessel, His vessel, an instrument He was going to use to speak to me. I was certain I was being told to let go of my prideful independence and self-sufficiency.

Who orchestrates our steps? Who had placed exactly *that* kind hearted, empathetic compassionate woman behind me in the line on this very day? Who had put it on her heart to make the offer? Did I forget so very easily that He had perfectly placed such strangers in my life before? An incredible spiritual lesson that I had come to believe while studying the Christian classic "Abandonment to Divine Providence" by Caussade with Jan Smith, a gifted bible teacher on Amelia Island in Florida, came to my mind. I had learned in that class that it serves a believer well to see through eyes that are able to say "It is the Lord" regarding *every single thing* that happens to them in their life, both the minute and the huge.

I gratefully and humbly accepted the twenty seven dollars from the kind stranger and sent it back to her via snail mail when I got home. On the way home in the car, I sheepishly apologized to the Lord for being such a fool, again. There was, however, a huge smile on my face as I acknowledged and felt His great love and care for me, even though it was *nothing that I had ever earned or deserved.* He did it because I am His child, and that is what He delights in doing.

"Therefore, as the elect of God, holy and dearly loved, clothe yourselves with a heart of mercy, kindness, humility, gentleness, and patience" (Col.3:12, NIV)) I would say that the generous stranger behind me in line that day was properly dressed in her spiritual garments, while I had failed to pay attention to what I "wore."

And, my guests arrived much later...hours later than expected. What foolish creatures we have the potential to be, and so much worse, when we have our eyes off of the Lord!

CHAPTER FOURTEEN

"In my distress I called upon the Lord, and cried to my
God for help; He heard my voice out of His temple, and
my cry for help before Him came into His ears"

Psalm 18:6 (ESV)

✝ *THE SUMMER OF 2018 WAS A VERY STRESSFUL* and difficult time for
my son Jared who was 38 years old at the time. He had landed
in hospital emergency rooms two or three times with severe alcohol
poisoning during that summer, at least once in full blown seizure.
It was a nightmare, and oh, how he suffered with this disease of sin.

He had done well keeping sober in the earlier part of the year, a
period of sobriety that had started in February and sustained until
around June or so. In February, he had desperately, with a
discouraging and despairing sense of defeat, agreed to live at Great
Rock Church's "Men of Valor in Training" program- *again*. He
always seemed to be able to remain sober while living there. Fully
aware now of his own repetitive backsliding into the physical
bondage and destruction of alcohol, this was a horrible time for him,
and re-entry into the church program he'd already been through
was indescribably humbling.

I was in wintering Florida at that time. Intentionally, only by
faith and through the power and aide of the Holy Spirit, I had
remained completely detached from these winter relapse events.
Mothers of the addicted, this is very counter intuitive to how we are

wired in the natural, but the Lord showered His mercy and compassion down on this sinner, me, and made possible what was impossible for me to do. I was finally trusting the Lord with my Jared- His Jared first. Completely. I was not the one who could deliver him.

I'm certain that Jared at least partially, if not fully, understood at some level within that at this stage of his life the alcoholism was surely going to kill him if he didn't seek more continuous help and support. He did know that salvation from what he was rested in God. I believe that. Yet it seemed to *me* that he often could *not* see that God works through whatever He chooses, and that the help He provides is not restricted to coming from within the walls of the church. They say alcoholism is a disease of denial however, and I witnessed my son often slip back into it. A moment's stumble is all that it takes for full relapse. It's one of the insane symptoms of the disease.

Jared had spent a very fruitful year participating in this stabilizing, faith based program back in 2013. He'd left it after one year, to marry a newcomer to the church, in January of 2014. She'd rented a lovely house near the church, and he caved to the temptation to be with a beautiful woman in a lovely home, and to try to live a more "normal" life. His sobriety was not sustained- quick and predictable relapse followed. Five rocky roller coaster years had passed since then, during which the marriage had blasted apart. Somewhere within himself he seemed, at times, to know he couldn't beat the alcoholism. He'd put on a veneer of strength however, and frequently fail to acknowledge that he could not maintain sobriety without intense daily help and support from the Holy Spirit- and fellowship with like- brothers who knew the Lord.

My own sin of pride was strongly embedded in my son. I do not know whether at this stage he had ever been able to fully admit that he was powerless over this sin, but that God was not. Like his mother who raised him, he seemed to think that he was able to accomplish, on his own, whatever he set his mind to. Yet, he now knew God, I had no doubt. I could see that he was a work in progress, as we all are. The Lord got him sober again while in living in this church work program in 2018- through work, men's ministry and fellowship, faithful church attendance, and intense study of God's word. About four to five months later, after some intense disagreement with a program "supervisor" over how the kitchen and food supply operated, he left that fine program again. He went to stay at a nearby hotel.

Jared knew he was very vulnerable to his fleshly weakness for alcohol and was fearful of relapse when he made the choice to pridefully leave the program because the "man in charge"(recently recovered himself) would not comply with how Jared desired to operate the kitchen. Jared was incredibly knowledgeable on nutrition, applying rigid nutritional principles to his diet almost obsessively, as a substitute for his alcohol focus. This was very helpful for him and as a person who'd worked closely with nicotine addicts in the nineties, I believed in the value of substitution when battling conditioned behaviors. I confess however that I may have raised the bar of healthy eating during his childhood to idolatry level. He was unwilling to comply with the lower standard at the recovery house. It seemed miraculous that a kindhearted soul, an authentic believer from his church named James, took him into his own home, a few nights after he'd stayed at the hotel. He had seen Jared walking back to the hotel after an evening church service called "Broken Chains". They subsequently started an internet business together, and things seemingly, on the surface went along alright, until James arrived home one day to find Jared severely inebriated, and gave him the boot.

The ensuing summer months were a time of back to back severe relapses punctuated with very short times of sobriety, post medical detox. I, for the most part, and only by clinging to my faith in our God and who He is, and to what He has promised His children, kept my hands off. That is right, dear mother of the addicted one reading this, *I did not take him in.* God did not need *my* help! I was certain that if He had any role at all for me in mind, He was more than capable of making it clear to me. I confess it was terribly frightening to accept that it was likely that Jared might drink himself to death. Somehow, God held me fast. *He kept me, as I was unable to keep myself.* God is faithful to those who lay their Isaac down on the altar as Abraham did.

Late in August that year there was one day when Jared called me from a seedy motel up on Route One in Peabody where he had been holed up drinking continuously for some period of days. He had once again come to the point where his choice was to either medically detox, or be found dead. He wanted to live. He asked for a ride to the North Shore Medical Center in Salem. I knew I was not breaking my promise to the Lord, which was to be still and let Him be in control of Jared's course, by providing this ride. Again, I had learned the very hard way to stay out of the Lord's way, leave my son on the altar, and trust Him do what He does in the lives of His children without my intervening with my own human ideas. This day I was spiritually certain that providing this kind of life saving transport as a life saving measure to my beloved son, who was asking for the *right kind of help* in this dire situation, was not against God's will. So I asked the Lord to steel me, and I went.

There was not a judgmental bone in my body when I entered that pitiful disaster of a motel room. It reeked of alcohol, despair, and imminent death. It was a glimpse of Satan's potential victory in my son's life. Empty liquor bottles were strewn around the room. He was in a bad state, vomiting non-stop, and self poisoned by the will of Satan. My heart was so broken to see and smell this vivid picture of the bondage my son was in, a life and death struggle between the fallen flesh and God's Spirit.

Reader, think about this. Is it not it *always* a life and death struggle between the enticement of sin and the life given through the Spirit-even in instances when our personal battlefields might not *appear* to our own faulty eyes to be so drastically severe and deadly as addiction? Our own spiritual battlefields may frequently *appear as if* they are more benign and less dangerous to our own eyes, through our own blurry vision, when we choose to evaluate ourselves *comparatively* to other's sin. We can be tempted through this comparing to believe the lie- that we are operating on the "higher end" (less deadly we think) of sin's range all while drowning in our "seemingly lesser sin." Sins such as lying, jealousy, impatience, unkindness, unforgiveness, laziness, coveting, boasting, seeking self glory, self focus, and tendency to judge others. That's just a short list.

We lean towards thinking that if we determine that we rank "better than many" on a sliding scale of sin, that surely this saves us! Do we *not understand* that the spiritual outcome remains the *same for all without Christ*? Spiritual death for eternity is the certain outcome of our inborn separation from God in the natural. The only solution is supernatural, spiritual. Our stubborn, persistent resistance to His will for us begets nothing except eternal separation from God. Without our Savior, the wages of sin is death! That specifically means spiritual death. Period. Jesus is the *only way*, sent as a gift from the Father to reconnect and restore us to Him!

Isn't it marvelous that there is a *Way*? *"Today, if you hear His voice, do not harden your hearts."* (Hebrews 3:15)

Does any reader still think you can be saved by perfect obedience to the law? Have you not read, do you not know, of the people's constant failure throughout all of history? What does it take to convince you, you who are depending on your own inability to live a good and Godly life?

It takes God's work. It takes your surrender to the same. Leave rebellion behind.

It was heart wrenching for me to see that my son's familiarity with this near death scenario, in his sickened and self poisoned state, enabled him to be matter of fact and routine about his need to be medically detoxed urgently. How he suffered. Still, it touched me how this very sinner clung so dogmatically to his faith. Alcoholics and addicts let me say this to you: Your flesh need not condemn you. Your flesh, your DNA, your "wicked" history need not define who you are, as this sinner's former life of choosing sin has not condemned her. I say the exact same to the person who believes they are living what the world perceives as a "good life", but has rejected Jesus. Your flesh need not condemn you! Jesus, who was *always* God's plan for salvation, who came to reconnect the Father's beloved children back to His heart, draws us into His family. He has covered us ALL.. but we need to *repent, believe and follow.* (John 3:15-16)

We also need to always recall that *mercy trumps judgment!* It is so very easy to forget this, and our own inner critical spirits love to rise up and pridefully parade *our own* judgment as Christ's righteousness! This is only a harmful masquerade of the true *Kingdom.* This is NOT okay with God! God is the *only* judge required or qualified, and we need to follow the directives of our Holy Judge and not attempt to take on *HIS* divine role. We need to regularly renew and pursue activities that will restore a Godly mindset within ourselves, because it is an innate common human tendency for us to judge and condemn others' sins that *appear* to be of a different or more serious kind than our own. We just decide that the other's sin is more severe and more spiritually damaging.

ALL OF IT leaves us separated permanently from God unless God in *His mercy reaches down and saves us!* The work is His, so we can not boast that we were or are able to earn *anything. It is always Him.* The glory is always to God! His grace changes everything! It transforms everything! It is He who works ALL within ALL!

"...for it is God who works in you to will and to act according to his good purpose."

Phil.2:13 (NIV)

From the motel on Route One, Jared asked me to take him to Beverly Hospital. The waiting room was full, however knowing that he had little time left before damaging seizures overtook him in the physical, he walked to the admissions desk and they rushed him in and started IV's. I stayed with him giving support and encouragement and reading scripture together for hours as the staff walking by looked at us as if we were crazy people be pitied. Then I departed.

He was sent to the Center for Addictive Behavior in Boston after this, but chose not to transfer to a longer treatment facility as suggested, when his detox, which takes many more days than most realize, was completed. He eventually landed on the streets of Boston, homeless, and seeking housing from shelters. Full relapse occurred yet again.

I reached out during this time to many brothers and sisters in Christ who are true prayer warriors, to pray in Jared's behalf. At church on that Sunday I sought extra prayer with a dear man, Peter, an associate pastor at the time, available at the front of my church that Sunday to pray with those brothers and sisters seeking personal prayer when the service ended. I texted my sister Diane and Kathy (whom I didn't want to share a room with years before) to pray also.

Laura and Sandy, dear sisters from my church, prayed. I know his brother in Christ Mathew Nadworny, the pastor from Great Rock church, prayed.

Many prayed.

A week or two passed, and one day, a Wednesday, I received a voicemail on my phone. It was from a counselor calling in behalf of my son. He was calling from a counselor's office at the Center for Addictive Behavior in Boston.

I called right back and Jared was still in his office. The counselor put him on the phone. Jared asked me if I could give him a ride to "The Dimock Center" in Roxbury, a long term treatment facility for individuals struggling with addiction, in two days, on that coming Friday morning. He had agreed this time to go there, to receive extended assistance and treatment, but would need transport from one facility to the other. The counselor had let him use the phone to call and ask me.

Relieved that he was still alive and in a place where practical help and support was available, and aware that I had no time to think over and pray regarding my answer, I quickly agreed to provide the ride. When I hung up the phone I did start to pray, asking the Lord for assurance that I was in *His* will and pleasing *Him* if I provided this ride. Only those who comprehend how damaging any form of enabling is in the setting of addiction can begin to understand my angst. You see, as I have said, the Lord had taught me to trust *Him and Him only* with the rescue of my son for many years now. I did trust Him, and had been most grateful and relieved to cast away this burden of human fear, anxiety and worry that tormented me. Surrendering the totality of my son's life to the Lord allowed me to breathe. *He and not I* could fix, redeem and restore. Mothers, in their eagerness to *fix*, are often in great danger of getting in the Lord's way and thwarting His plans for

His adult children. For years now I had practiced this Godly principle of detachment, handing my son over to God, with intermittent spiritual success. It was very hard. I confess I sometimes relapsed by falling into grieving or depression and that does not reflect the power of God's Spirit in me. I believe this practice of *handing over* was saving *me*- protecting my mental health, allowing me to retain a measure of emotional steadfastness, allowing me to taste unexpected peace, and simultaneously clearing the way for the work of the Lord to take effect and blossom in my son's life. And mine.

That is why I was completely obsessed over being diligent not to be cavalier over extending *any kind* of my own efforts other than fervent prayer, to my son. I either trusted God with him, or I didn't. There is no "Ya, but...." or "But if *I* only"...He can do it without you, mother reading this. Or dad. He is the One who is *able. The One and Only. Do you believe it? Can you remove your hands?* I assure you, you can not remove your hands, without the strength of Christ imparted upon you. This will come via faith.

Faith comes by knowing (hearing, reading) God's word and having your Spiritual eyes opened by the Spirit to learn from the experiences provided for His dear ones. Are you indwelled by the Holy Spirit of God? We can come to know Him experiencially when we surrender to and believe in and are alert to and watching for the Power of our Christ's resurrection. We may expect it, but only in God's timing-not by demand. The power of God is available to all who *believe* that Christ died for them, once, and for *all.*

On Friday morning as I left my home in Gloucester and drove down Route 93 South, I was inwardly experiencing an intense spiritual struggle. Was my Father displeased with me? There was much trepidation in my heart created by my uncertainty as to whether or not I was acting in accordance with my Father's will. I was pleading with the Lord to provide to me a sign or indication to either affirm that this task was in alignment with what He wanted me to do, or to make clear my departure from His will. The ugly, insane things Jared had spewed to me the week before during his inebriated state were clearly evidence of "the old former man" controlling him. I needed and wanted to keep way clear of that type of assault, as commanded by the Lord- while Jared learned to work out his own salvation. I knew this was a right choice, and the will of God for me to guard my beaten up and trodden on heart.

During my prayer and crying out while driving, my attention caught on the license plate on the car in front of me. It read "GAL218." Now, what Christian doesn't know where to go with that? That vehicle remained in front of me until I turned off onto my exit. Galatians 2:20 is one of my favorite verses but I could not recall what the verse just two lines ahead of it said! I knew in my spirit that without doubt that whatever it said, it was a word from the Lord and I was to deliver it to Jared.

When I arrived at given address, I had to park on Mass Avenue. Well, this was at nine am in Boston on a weekday morning! I felt the hand of the Lord on me and along with that His intervention in my behalf, as a car pulled out of a parking spot at a meter a very short distance up the street from the Boston Center for Addictive Behavior. Perfect timing. If any reader is familiar with this kind of Boston crazy traffic, they can understand that quickly obtaining a parking space in this area seemed like a little miracle in itself. Our Lord is behind *all things that happen!* I was grateful that He did not seem to be showing me obstacles, but helping.

A short while after my son was in the car with me, and we were on our way to the Dimock Center, the Holy Spirit brought it to my remembrance to tell him to look up the verse that I had been shown on the license plate. I told Jared prior to his reading it that I believed it was a word for him, whatever it may be. I asked him if he would mind reading it aloud, as I too was curious to know what it was the Lord was saying.

"For if I rebuild what I tore down, I prove myself to be a transgressor." (Galatians 2:18 ESV) -read my son aloud.

This admonition was given to Peter from Paul, when Paul noticed that Peter was setting an unchristian example by *reverting* back to eating *only* with Jews again- some high ranking ones within the Jewish religious hierarchy. He was suddenly "chickening out"- trying to please Jewish leaders at the expense of ignoring God's teaching! Jesus had taught the apostles that eating with Gentiles was just fine, and that the law wasn't a means by which anyone could obtain salvation.

This incident had occurred *after* Peter accepted God's former teaching given to him through a dream. Grace now bestowed because of his Lord Christ Jesus's work had done away with the need for Peter (and us) to strive on one's own to keep the law. He *knew* he could eat with Gentiles without offending God, and that acting on that knowledge pleased God! Peter, by doing this now, was publicly denying the grace which begets freedom in Christ. His actions weren't consistent with believing that Christ's perfect life, death and resurrection had fulfilled the law. It appeared to onlookers as if he was once again believing that *keeping* the law *was* mandatory for salvation! It looked as though he did not understand God's truth- that the Spirit of life, through Christ Jesus, had freed him from the law of sin and death. (you too dear reader) Peter struggled with accepting that all foods were now considered clean, Jewish eating rituals no longer required-and the false idol of "what will people think?!" He was ignoring the new covenant of grace, which had replaced the old covenant. His actions weren't consistent with his understanding that people themselves aren't ever spiritually *clean* unless cleansed by the blood of Jesus through faith!

No amount of hand washing or eating rituals can make us righteous! Our *only option for redemption and Godliness is to bow one's head and allow Jesus to bestow His righteousness upon us and within us.* It is *His.*

Peter was obviously fearful of the condemnation of the pro-circumcision group of powerful Jewish men. Under self pressure to not invite their wrath upon him, he was being a hypocrite. That's right-our *PETER!* Can you believe it? Paul rebuked him for this and made a powerful point...that, we are *all* eventually law breakers in one way or another, transgressors by nature, often knowing *what* to do or *not do* and then choosing the wrong thing. Everyone is in desperate need of *grace.* Only the blood of Jesus covers our sin. We can not do it. We can not act our way out of it and satisfy God on our own. Sin has crippled us all.

We need our Messiah. There is no other remedy for what we are. If you are aware of what you are in your deeper being, then you know that these words are true.

Our Savior is needed continuously by all of us while we live in this earthly realm, *even after salvation.* He is a daily need, our God.

I write again, we *can not conquer sin.* Does not Paul cry out in Roman's chapter seven "What a wretched man I am! Who will rescue me from this body of death?" (Romans 7:24 NIV) The same sorrowful cry of repeated failure could have been Peter's that day, as he caved into fear of disapproval and rejection by powerful Jewish men, and relapsed back into his old ways.

Does not the rich young ruler in Mark 10:17 seek to be a perfect law KEEPER in the hope to obtain heaven through his own strength and works? *And Jesus loved him.* What mercy we find in our Jesus! What a patient teacher is our Jesus! This man did not yet comprehend his own *total inability* to accomplish reconciliation to the Father, through sufficient law keeping and works; as distinguished from simply harboring a believing saving faith in the teachings and sufficiency of Jesus. How I hope we meet this motivated but unable young man in heaven! We have much in common with him! The word does not tell us if we will, but I think it likely! The rich young man was interested in earning eternal life for himself, and by himself. Jesus made it clear to him that it was *not he who could do it.* As love filled Jesus's heart for this person just before He told him something he *would* have to do to achieve his goal on his own- that he *knew* the man to be incapable of doing (give away all his riches)...He had nothing but *love for him.* Do you know His message to us is the *same?*

Peter was incapable! Paul was incapable! Moses was incapable! Jacob and Joshua were both incapable! The list of incapable saints in the Bible goes on and on. The young rich ruler was incapable too, but Jesus. "But Jesus" for every one! In the same conversation, right after the rich young ruler walks away very deflated and troubled, Jesus assures his confused disciples who are now wondering who, if anyone, can be saved. He tells them "With man this is impossible, but not with God; all things are possible with God." (Mark 10:27 NIV)

Thus, dear reader, I pray that each of us surrenders our belief that there is some way that we may obtain heaven by any work on our own. May every one come to recognize and trust and lean on our Jesus Who will in response and with merciful love, bring us at last, at last, at last through those pearly gates. If they are indeed pearly! I can't wait to find out! What I know for certain is that heaven is beyond that of which my mind is able to conceive.

After reading Galatians 2:18 aloud, these words of scripture regarding what we all seem to ultimately do to prove we are by nature indeed useless transgressors- my son Jared was startled at how they completely aligned with his personal circumstances. Had he not once again proved himself to be a *transgressor?* A transgressor differs from the sinner who has not heard the gospel or of the law, sees no need for repentance, and thus sins. A transgressor knows the gospel, knows the law, recognizes the truth and wonder of each, at least to some degree, yet will always eventually buckle under sooner or later when operating in his own strength. Should we be surprised to discover, that just as Peter and Paul were in their flesh, we are transgressors too? May I say we are in good company? Whether or not knowing that we regularly transgress leads to despair, is proportional to the depth and steadfastness of our belief that the power of the blood of Jesus is sufficient to save His flock.

As for me, He has put me in the wagon of hope on a trail of suffering and trials leading to heaven. He enables me to abide with acceptance and inner spiritual joy. He has made me a citizen of His kingdom and as He accomplishes through grace, both my part and His, I can often hardly breathe; as I could hardly breathe at the moment in the car following Jared reading the verse aloud. I was once again inwardly astounded, as I drove home after dropping my son at the long term recovery hospital. I realized how the Lord He had spoken to me and to Jared so clearly, that very morning.

We thank you Lord for your relentless faithful pursuit of us who are wired in the natural to be ungodly! We are so grateful that it is *You* who never fails.

❖   ❖   ❖

"So, my brothers, you also died to the law through the body of Christ that you might belong to another, to him who was raised from the dead in order that we might bear fruit to God. For when we were controlled by the sinful nature, the sinful passions aroused by the law were at work in our bodies, so that we bore fruit for death. But now, by dying to what once bound us, we have been released from the (good and holy*) law so that we serve in the new way of the Spirit, and not in the old way of the written code."

Romans 7:4-6 (NIV)

(*"good and holy" inserted by writer)

"And call upon me in the day of trouble; I shall rescue you, and you will honor Me"

Psalm 50:15 (CSB)

CHAPTER FIFTEEN

"Whoever has my commands and obeys them, he is the
one who loves me. He who loves me will be loved by my
Father, and I too will love him and *show myself to him.*"

John 14:21, (NIV;
emphasis by author)

✟ MY MOTHER EVELYN WENT TO BE WITH the Lord at the age of 85
years old. She had a terrible time of it with vascular dementia
during the last few years of her life, and those symptoms had
exacerbated and then accelerated rapidly in the last several months
of her life. As her brain was progressively damaged she suffered
with extreme paranoid psychotic hallucinations and delusions,
during her last seven to eight weeks of being in her body. When she
stopped eating we had her transferred from the hospital's eldercare
psych unit in Lynn Massachusetts to the Kaplan House in Danvers,
for hospice care. We experienced it to be a lovely place of tender,
merciful physical care and comfort for the dying.

It was there she finally slipped away from this world here, to
her eternal reward where she is now, no doubt with the Lord. This
happened on Sunday night November 23rd at about 7:22 p.m. with
myself, my one living sister Diane, and my husband Curt by her
bedside.

The day following her death, Monday, my sister and I agreed to
meet at my mother's now empty home, leave one of our cars parked

there, and go out and about together to make all the many funeral arrangements. This included arranging all the details with the funeral home, and the arrangements with Spinelli's where we as the bereaved daughters would hostess the interment luncheon for family and friends. That we did, and with only one break for lunch it took us most of the day to accomplish everything. Having completed all of our "to do" list we arrived back at 546 Lynnfield Street Street, our childhood home, much later in the day, and went inside together. We took care of some practical issues that needed to be addressed there, including digging through more photos to select for display during the services at the funeral home, later in the week. Finally, we were ready to depart and head back to our separate homes, Diane's on the South Shore of Boston in Raynham, and mine in Gloucester. We were bone weary, grieving, and emotionally spent. It was just shy of twenty four hours since our mother's departure.

One of us, I recall not who, had her hand on the kitchen back door to open it so we could both leave together. We agreed to reconvene the next day for a meeting with my mother's pastor who was mine also, at that time. Suddenly, I remembered I had forgotten to check for our mother's mail, and bring it inside. "Oh wait Diane, I said, I want to go take mum's mail out of the foyer and bring it inside."

Thus we went back through the house, and I swooped up about a dozen pieces of mail from the floor of the front foyer where it had all fallen when the postman pushed it through the slot. Diane followed me as I walked into the dining room, tossed it all onto the table, and began to quickly separate the "throwaways" from the important.

I can not explain to you what happened next, except that Diane and I knew with our whole hearts and souls that it was "from the Lord."

We both heard distinct music. Our eyes met with wonderment, each one silently asking with her eyes "do you hear what I hear?" The music was coming from the living room which was behind us. The tune was "rock-a-bye-baby." In surreal breath holding amazement, we walked towards it. We stopped short of the large piece of wooden furniture, which not only held our mother's television, but also had a built in, attractive cabinet with a glass door, attached to the left of the television shelf. The music came from within that.

We opened the glass door, and there was the beautiful musical statue that our deceased sister Janice had given to our mother prior to her own death from breast cancer, back in 1996. The statue was of a mother leaning lovingly over a cradle, tending to her baby within. I had forgotten all about that beautiful gift until now, as my mother had eventually apparently tucked it inside this cabinet, and it was towards the back, out of daily sight unless one opened the door and peered in.

"Rock-a bye-baby-on- the- tree- top-when-the-wind-blows-the-cradle-will-rock" the musical tune twinkled away as the statue and cradle rotated. We watched it, that perfect portrait of a mother loving and comforting her baby as the wind blew. (is this also a portrait of God's provision of comfort?)When it ceased rotating and playing, now silent, we picked it up in awe. It had played for a prolonged time, not just for a few leftover unwound notes! Our older sister Janice had been gone now for eighteen years. Never, ever, to either of our knowledge, had that musical statue played spontaneously before. Our mother's illness had mandated that other people, especially myself (since I lived closest) and another hired woman caretaker named Irma, spend *much* time in the home with her during her last few years of life. *This spontaneous music had not ever occurred. Nor has it ever repeated itself in the ensuing five years as it sits on a shelf in my own home in Gloucester.* No, it had happened this *one time,* while both of us were present together in the home, approximately twenty four hours after our mother's death.

Diane and I walked out of our childhood home with great joy and wonder filling our hearts that evening. We both could not *believe* what had just happened, yet, we were *both there* and we *did* believe it. We were certain of the following three things, albeit we can not explain it further.

A message bearing tender, extraordinary comfort and love had been delivered from the Lord to two of His daughters, in an incredible way, and in His perfect timing; a supernatural event had occurred for our spiritual good, and edification of our faith in the one living God; our Holy Father was with us then at that moment, always, and we were to let others know of the event, that glory might be brought to His Holy Name.

Every believer has to know "it is the Lord!"Do you see it reader? If not, then ask the Lord to remove your heart of stone and make it flesh.

The next day when we were with Pastor Mat Nadworny of Great Rock Church in Danvers for the purpose of planning the order of the service, he too expressed wonder when we reported to him what the Lord had done for us. We even all laughed a bit when he he said with admitted envy "why doesn't stuff like that ever happen to me?!" I reminded him gently that he had told me that he had been given the gift of tongues.

Thank you again Father, that You divinely engineered those wondrous moments for my sister Diane and I in our time of loss and sorrow.

"Blessed are they who mourn, for they will be comforted."

Matthew 5:4 (NIV)

CHAPTER SIXTEEN

"Be devoted to one another in brotherly love. Honor one another above yourselves. Never be lacking in zeal, but keep your spiritual fervor, serving the Lord. Be joyful in hope, patient in affliction, faithful in prayer."

Romans 12:10-12 (NIV)

DURING THE WINTER OF *2019*, while my husband Curt and I were staying in Florida for the season in order to escape the New England snow and ice, I felt prompted to reach out and write to a very dear eighty eight year old saint from my home church named Georgie. This dear man had made a point of befriending me starting the very first time I presented at that wonderful church, the Orthodox Congregational Church of Lanesville, MA. He was eighty five years old when we first met, and suffering with advanced prostate cancer. Despite his infirmity, weakness, and painful challenges with ambulating, he and his wife Betty seldom missed a service. Georgie's faithfulness and zeal for scripture penetrated my soul, and drew me in return to relish being his friend. He'd written poetry and music during his lifetime, and all of that which I was blessed to hear or read brought glory to the Lord. I was fearing that I might not get to see him in the flesh again (although he was still alive upon my return from Florida) and I did not want to lose the opportunity to know him better, and encourage him in any way the Lord would allow me to.

Thus I began to cultivate ongoing e-mail communication (the modern version of "pen pal"!) with this old man and brother in the faith that I so admired for his *zeal* in fervently pursuing the wisdom and holy knowledge found in scripture. Our communication went back and forth, and I do believe we edified one another along the way. Below are some excerpts from this dear man's last written email message to me, written shortly before his death. May you be edified by reading this following portion, as you call to mind that this man was not only on the cusp of his own his own physical death when he wrote this, keenly aware of it's imminence, but that he and his wife Betty had recently endured the wrenching loss of one of their daughters only several months before, to cancer.

Oh, my sweet friend Melody,

This e-mail is probably the most difficult for me to respond to of all I have ever received. God has changed my outlook regarding my scarcity of Gospel knowledge and I don't always understand what He's trying to convey to this inner man except that He's preparing my spirit for the ultimate transition awaiting me as I enter His glorious presence!

So my feeling is that He has led me to (*name of teacher left out) as His chosen conduit of spiritual education to better equip me for my final Jordan crossing entering into a promised land that exceeds my wildest expectations filled with a love that, as of now, for me is incomprehensible!

(portion of Georgie's discussion of the significance of the ram in the thicket from Genesis 22:13 is left out here)

I agree, our amazement is certainly to be savored over and over again. How can you not love a God that is such a bountiful supplier covering such a broad eternal expanse. Wheeew!!!!

At this point in time my goal is to try to the best of my ability(as my God supplies) to attend church as often as I can. Last Sunday I was visited by Sallie May before the service and after the service by what I kinda feel is our little core group. I have experienced a lot of receptivity to the things that I have learned and respect everyone's right to disagree. I'm in the same folder with Susan who acknowledges that she likes being wrong as that's a fabulous way to learn. I find myself praying nightly that God will generate a humble attitude in my heart as I'm so aware that shooting off my mouth can shine a light on a totally different pathway that can so easily turn people off big time. Of course I realize that I need to constantly remind myself that I am a privileged recipient of gems that can only emanate from the Holy Spirit from whom I often feel that I experience a void regarding His unconditional control (how I long for that)!!

Thank you for your prayer that reminds me of how important it is for me to get my eyes off of myself and approach our loving Father in full surrender mode. Don't let me forget how much safety is found in those Everlasting Arms.

Thanks so much for your undeserved encouragement and may your life be filled with blessings from God's inexhaustible supply.

Leaning on Him and Him only.

Georgie

Georgie's focus was on his zealousness for the Lord, and for spiritual growth as long as he was here and not there (where he is now). I witnessed a smile on his face off and on as he lay in a semi comatose state for several days, at the hospice facility where he died. That is a man of faith, friend. He was so happy and excited to depart! I'd only been privileged to witness this countenance once before in my life, when my dear believing cousin Gerry Cole joyfully received the last rites as she lay dying from cancer.(a tradition of her church)

Needless to say, I treasured the spiritual connection with Georgie that the Lord had gifted me with. I looked forward to receiving his messages. Thus, when he recommended in one e-mail that I listen to a particular evangelical minister, a writer and Bible teacher from the UK who is widely known and heard on various broadcasts and U TUBE videos, I was eager to hear him for myself. I wanted to explore whether or not this was one of the teachers the Lord had on His list for *my* edification. He has often used other believers to lead me to something that would edify my spirit. I believed that if Georgie had benefited from this man's teachings, then perhaps I would too.

Well, because of my two past divorces, and knowing this is not God's will for His children, as I looked over the titles of the many U TUBE teachings by this pastor, I chose to listen to one in which he taught on divorce and remarriage. I was devastated, and terribly blown away with horror as I listened to this particular teaching! The unnamed pastor presented a very legalistic, merciless message on this matter. He taught that if a woman was divorced and had remarried, that not only was she an adulteress, but that she had no *no hope* of heaven. Now of course that would actually be true for those who expect to get to heaven on their own accord, by trying to keep the law perfectly or at least "enough" they reason, to gain entry into the Kingdom. However, it deletes the doctrine of grace. In this preacher's view, the scriptures absolutely said that a divorced and remarried woman could not be in the Kingdom, because she was an adulteress. He came at it with the attitude of "Sorry people but God is serious about what He says to do and don't do, so you remarried women are not off the hook. You are *out.*" He drove his point home relentlessly. He spewed condemnation. After listening to him however, on this particular day, I felt as if I had been spiritually shattered.

At the same time, on the same day that I was wrestling internally with what this generally well respected pastor's teaching taught, and what it meant for me if *he* was accurate, I also had started to question the wisdom of my own spontaneous behavior in my CBS (Christian Bible Study) group that very morning. Thus there were *two* troublesome, distressful matters inwardly eating away at me simultaneously. Satan attacked.

During my CBS morning's group discussion I had confessed, talked about, a person in my life for whom I had hateful feelings that I was completely unable to reign in, on my own. I confessed to the ladies that I had completely failed at being able to change how I felt towards this person, in any way. Those feelings persisted and sometimes consumed me, displacing anything that was good, noble, lovely or pure (of Christ) in my mind. I often felt helpless against my low simmering anger towards the person. I had quite vehemently used the word "hate" when confessing this to the dear ladies who were seeking to grow in the Lord along with me, as I told them about this person and my uncontrollable dislike that often owned me.

So even prior to listening to the extremely disturbing U Tube message from Georgie's favored pastor, earlier that same afternoon, I was already experiencing internal conflict regarding my own lack of good judgment in using such a powerful word as "hate" in my personal confession to the group of women. I cared about them, and was horrified that I may have been a negative influence. I feared that my passionate and careless expression of dislike could potentially render some kind of soul damage to one of them. Had I been spiritually reckless in expressing and demonstrating through my voice tone my unchristian emotional posture towards this person? Could one of the younger women be harmed by hearing such a venomous outcry from one older than she, who claimed to be a daughter of the Most High? Had I modeled a condition of Satan being in control of my heart and mind and left anyone thinking that *that* was an "okay" way to feel? It's obviously not fruit of the Spirit being poured forth. My conscience would not let me rest. I felt an extreme reactive depression from what I'd spoken that morning.

So with these two matters eating away at my inner core, I went to bed that night, one spring evening in the April of 2019, and did not sleep. I had no peace, only torment, as Satan continued his evil work in my mind. I was quite certain I had caused harm to sisters in Christ, been a terrible example, and of course that made sense because nothing about me was of the Lord! I was a condemned adulteress, in a marriage of adultery, with no hope of being part of the Kingdom of God. I was useless and hopeless, unqualified to ever be a mature role model or an encourager to younger Christian women.

Dear one, can you perceive the viciousness of Satan's attack in my mind in this scenario? Believer, can you imagine my dismay? My life was and is Christ. I lay there and listened to Satan messing with my mind, and rattling me further as he gleefully condemned me. After very little sleep I arose on Thursday, and my husband went off to play tennis. After Curt left, I was on my knees in our living room, full of despair and crying out for the Lord to speak truth to me. It is hard for me to describe to you how deeply and painfully distressed I was. If I had no hope of heaven because of my past and current sin, and my life was not a contribution to the Kingdom in any way...where was I to go? I had no where to go. My life was meaningless. (John 6:68) I bought the lie.

As I wept and anguished in prayer, I felt the Lord speak to my heart as he began to unravel the mess of confusion and grief dominating me, and imparted to me His clarity, in the midst of my painful confusion. He clearly spoke to my heart and said "STAND."

I literally stood as commanded, and listened. He reminded me that there is "no condemnation in Christ." (Romans 8:1) He reminded me that Christ had kept the law perfectly in my behalf. What sinner can keep the law? None, there is not one who keeps it perfectly. It is faith that saves. He showed me that the pastor on UTUBE had the spirit of an unmerciful pharisee as he preached to God's people that they themselves must keep the law in order to be saved. That is false. A calm flooded through my being as enlightenment in the truth did also, and at that *exact moment, while obediently standing, my phone beeped.* My eyes flickered over to the couch in front of me, where it lay. I did not recognize the number, but there on the screen was Jeremiah 29:11.

"For I know the plans I have for you" declares the Lord, "plans to prosper you and not to harm you, plans to give you hope and a future."

(NIV)

That scripture goes on to say,

"Then you will call upon me and come to pray to me, and

I will listen to you. You will seek me and find me when
you seek me with all your heart."

(NIV)

I knew the message was clearly from the Lord, but I was curious
of course to see whom He had used as His instrument to speak
through, to me. It turned out to be a precious saint from my CBS
(Christian Bible Study) class named Elaine, a true sister in the faith.
She had never personally texted me before, ever. Yet, on this
particular morning, at this exact time, she felt prompted to send me
what she was unaware was a scripture so very dear to my heart,
that God had used with me over and over again through the years.

Dear reader, if you have not yet heard the Lord speak quietly to
you in your heart, if He has never told you that you belong to Him
and may STAND in His sight because you follow Jesus, I implore
you to seek *more* and to *cry out* for Him to show you what His
written truth means. An anointed beloved Bible teacher of mine I
am blessed to study with, named Jan Smith on Amelia Island at the
Plantation Chapel, implores all who read God's word to pray
beforehand for the Spirit to reveal more to their believing mind
every time they seek truth there. I have discovered this is priceless
advice! The Spirit will do it!

Thank you Lord for sisters and brothers that recognize and
respond to the Spirit within them! Later that same day of my
experience aforementioned, I shared with precious Elaine my
gratitude that she had acted upon the quiet voice within her. It was
my hope that she would be edified by the miraculous perfect timing
and scripture choice also. Lord, may we never miss the
opportunities you provide to each saint.

❋ ❋ ❋

"Therefore, put on the full armor of God, so that when the day of evil comes, you may be able to stand your ground, and after you have done everything, to stand."

Ephesians 6:13 (NIV)

"Who are you to judge someone else's servant? To their own master, servants stand or fall. And they will stand, for the Lord is able to make them stand."

Romans14:4 (NIV)

"Whom have I in heaven but you? And earth has nothing I desire besides you."

Psalm 73:25 (NIV)

"When they kept on questioning him, he straightened up and said to them, "Let anyone of you who is without sin be the first to throw a stone at her."Again he stooped down and wrote on the ground. At this, those who heard began to go away one at a time, the older ones first, until only Jesus was left, with the woman still standing there. "Woman, where are they? Has no one condemned you?" "No one, sir," she said. "Then neither do I condemn you" Jesus declared. "Go now and leave your life of sin."

When Jesus spoke again to the people he said, "I am the light of the world. Whoever follows me will never walk in darkness but will have the light of life."

John 8:7-12 (NIV)

CHAPTER SEVENTEEN

"Have I not commanded you? Be strong and courageous.
Do not be afraid; do not be discouraged, for the Lord
your God will be with you wherever you go."

Joshua 1:9 (NIV)

✟ IT IS THURSDAY MORNING, March 4th, 2020. Curt and I are in
Florida living as "snowbirds" at this time of year. On this
particular morning we have three unexpected guests with us who
had arrived about eight thirty p.m. the evening before. Two of
them are our grandson Curtis, twenty one, and granddaughter
Megan, almost twenty three. They are Curt's daughter's children.
Megan also has a little daughter, Everlee, our great granddaughter,
who is two.

The visit was unexpected, a surprise, having been unplanned.
They had decided not to let us know they were coming before
leaving their home state. I confess I am *not* a spontaneous person by
nature, and it had taken me a few long minutes after the initial call
the day before, Wednesday, when I was told their arrival was
imminent, to process "the surprise." They had decided during the
last leg of their car trip from Massachusetts to Amelia Island Florida
that they should tell us about their plans to come and stay. I was
also expecting two other guests to arrive that Friday evening, for a
long weekend. I had enjoyed preparing for them, having had their
visit on our calendar for months, my own selfish preference for

receiving guests, yes, even when they're family. (This was Curt's daughter Erin with her husband Matt) Two guests jumping up to five and with only one extra bedroom momentarily overwhelmed me; that's just how I am in the flesh. I love extending hospitality but fail completely with spontaneity. Perhaps some of my readers might relate to my struggle with being spontaneously flexible? It's a personality thing I believe. I wasn't brought up by parents who were gifted with the ability to be spontaneous, so I can self analyze I suppose and see the "nurture" piece effect playing out in myself. There are my sorry and useless excuses for not being prepared to see the Lord's divine orchestration behind *all things* in the lives of His beloved kids.

The Lord Himself did a quick work within me to change my heart during Curtis's initial phone call to me on Wednesday while they were still on the road, but just hours away. He brought to my mind a powerful teaching from my Florida Bible study on "Abandonment to Divine Providence" a Christian classic by Caussaude. He teaches that as Christians we need to learn to say and believe, no matter what the circumstance or "seeming" inconvenience, that "it is the Lord." In fact, Caussaude teaches that in the big picture of faith, Satan is nothing more than God's errand boy when it comes to His children- just a means by which He can and *will* accomplish His desired outcome. With that amazing truth in mind, a truth I believed with all my being, my attitude quickly was changed by the Lord (I take no credit) and I embraced the idea of having them *all* here at once, and disregarded my flesh which relentlessly campaigned daily to be the entity in control of my life. (and still does)

So on this Thursday morning Curt and I are playing with the baby Everlee, and enjoying our interactions with Curtis and Megan. We are much more than "making the best of it". Curt and I are happy, very happy in the moment. I chuckle inwardly as I recall an "old woman" from years ago that would have stoked the fire in her heart as I framed this as an "inconvenience" with a martyr type attitude, told all my close friends how disrespectful the grand kiddos whom I love (very much) had been, (and of course because they weren't raised "correctly" etc etc)...do you get the *ugly sinful* picture of my heart condition? I had personally been that carnally driven person, for a long time, in James 3, from whose mouth sprang salt and fresh water. It's wrong. That is offensive to the Father I claim to love, and do love with all my mind, heart, strength, and soul. It was way past time to stop that behavior and apply the spirit of understanding imparted to me, and act accordingly upon my belief in the wise words in James 3:

"The tongue is a fire, a world of evil. Placed among the parts of our bodies, the tongue contaminates the whole body and sets on fire the course of life, and is itself set on fire by hell."

James 3:6 (NIV)

"but no human being can contain the tongue. It is a restless evil, full of deadly poison."

James 3:8 (ESV))

"From the same mouth comes blessing and cursing. It should not be like this my brothers. A spring can not pour both fresh and brackish water from the same opening, can it?"

James 3:11 (ISV)

It perpetually lifts my heart and gives me great encouragement when God shows me in any moment the difference between something He is equipping me to do through Christ in the present moment, that which I never could *never* have "risen to" without Christ in me, and the natural corrupted me. I use the word "risen" very intentionally, because He rises me away from the death of my sin when I am willing to be taken out of it by His hand, and then filled with His life instead of my useless, hopeless one. His becomes mine, and which is eternal and glorious. This is a brief example of the exchanged life...our carnal and condemned one, left behind in the dust intentionally, so His Spiritual and righteous one may replace it. It appears. It is a supernatural activity and glorifies God. Colossians 3:3-4 says

"For you died, and your life is now hidden with Christ in God. When Christ, who is your life, appears, then you will also appear with him in glory."

(NIV)

This happens any time we die to self (desire and direction) and let Christ live through us in any given moment.

Over the years, I have often noted that after great spiritual victory in Christ there often follows strong spiritual attack. I have no doubt that many believers who read this have noted the same.

Curt, myself, Curtis, Megan, and two year old Everlee later in the morning wander down to the beach just to enjoy the whole beach ambiance, and watch the baby explore. It is relaxing and enjoyable. It's rare time spent together, because we don't see these older grandchildren very much anymore like we did continuously when they were younger. Thus is the flow of life.

My i-phone rings and I walk away from the noise of the waves so I can hear who it is. When I hear a gentleman on the other end asking me "Hello mam, do you know Jared Mancinelli" my heart freezes and time stops for a moment as I greatly fear his potential next words. For many months now, perhaps even a few years, I have dreaded that I could perhaps receive a call one day to inform me that he was found dead from his alcoholism.

Thanks to the Lord the unknown man doesn't say that. After I confirm to him that I am Jared's mother, he tells me that he is the manager of a hotel called Yotel in Boston, which is not far from where my son lives. His name is Jeff Keanes, a manager there. He explains that they are "familiar" with Jared, and that he recalls Jared having stayed there the previous October, and having much "trouble." (October of 2019 Jared was taken from there to Mass General for alcohol detox, kept at the hospital under a Section 12, and then on the strong council of his Mass General addiction councilor Jonathan I had gone into Boston Municipal Court to complete a Section 35 to have him apprehended at discharge, and committed to a longer term facility in the hope of extending his physical life.)

Jared has developed a pattern in the past year or so of fleeing to this nearby hotel from his apartment, when he is having psychotic delusions and hallucinations from alcohol overdose. The reason he "flees" is that sadly, his delusions often include one where there are "many flying spiders all throughout his apartment" and in his mind, they keep biting him. He then takes off to stay at the hotel to escape his delusion of his apartment infested with flying, biting spiders. This is why he is known to Jeff.

On this morning Jeff tells me that he and other staff are very concerned for Jared's life. He tells me they had made a decision to have the police come and get him and bring him to the hospital, as he is "in a very bad way." Unfortunately, Jared had stumbled out of the hotel only moments before, and thus Jeff decided to call *me* because apparently he was "so badly off" that Jeff realized he was in desperate need of urgent assistance. His concern precipitated and motivated his trying to reach out to a family member, and that ended up being me of course, the mother, who only through total dependence on Christ's strength had not been in touch with Jared for ten weeks. I'd enjoyed a peace that surpassed all understanding during that time, believing with all my heart that the Lord was going to finish the work He had begun in Jared and that he did not require my assistance to do so.

You see, I had intentionally not initiated any contact at all with my son since about the second week of December or so. After two very bad phone calls spaced several days apart, I could not take the destruction that Jared's drunken hurtful words assaulted my heart with. Perhaps I could say they were Satan's words, coming at me through my son who was in an extremely weakened and ungodly state of fleshly reign, albeit I did not doubt he was one of God's saved children, a brother in Christ. I was not equipped to withstand this type of attack, unless...I *finally* understood I must *die* to my natural motherly reactions which prompt a mother to soothe and try to fix.. which is not what the Lord wants us to do when a man is forty. By staying in willing communication with him and allowing this drunken version of him access to my heart, I felt I was giving Satan a direct pathway for his poisoned grenades constructed by Jared's words, conceived in the bondage of alcoholism, to enter the inner chamber of my soul and render deep destruction.

"Guard your heart" flowed into my conscious mind in December 2019. Once again, I re-committed myself to trusting my Almighty God with my most precious gift of an only son, surrendering my helplessness and anguish to God's love and power.

I did tell Jared that he was welcome to call me any time he managed to get sober again, and that I hoped he would. The peace of heart that God imparted to me in the ensuing months was deeper than at any other previous time. I had made the decision to anchor my hope and serenity to Whom and What my God is, and not to my beloved son's state of sobriety or lack thereof. I renewed my intention to be obedient to the instructive God gives us through Paul, which is to focus on that which is true, noble, right, pure, lovely and admirable. (Philippians 4:8) Neither alcoholism, nor my own fears which rested in the knowledge of what *I could do to fix and restore, which is nothing at all*, came under the umbrella of those divinely inspired words.

Here I was, after almost three divinely provided peaceful months of being "held fast" by God's power, now being made aware *again* of the ongoing *DISASTER* of what Jared's disease of his flesh was rendering. It was right in my face all over again, yet this had not come about through any intention on my part or disobedient action to what I felt God had been saying to me these past months. (hands off Melody) I had not broken my vow to God to turn Jared *completely over* to His love and care, as Abraham did Isaac, by caving in and checking in(and checking in and checking in) on my son. How would *that* be trusting God to return my son to me well—if it was indeed His will? I figured then that the Lord must *want* me to know, and had put it into Jeff's heart to call me, for whatever purposes He had.

I gave Jeff a brief summary of how advanced Jared's alcoholism was, and told him that it was reasonable to believe that it was possible that he may not survive this current relapse. Jeff wanted to go after him, and find him! With a mixture of extreme weariness of heart, combined with living pulsating hope of the brand only known to a believing mother, I affirmed to Jeff how much that would mean to me, and perhaps might be helpful to Jared. (It is worthy to note that the following week Jeff called me to follow up and see how Jared had fared. I asked him what had prompted him to "go the extra mile" and take it upon himself to pursue a "drunk" stumbling out of his hotel. He replied "I knew this man must have a family who loved him".)

Love? Love, yes, I suppose, for sure. It was hanging by a divine thread after taking so many severe beatings throughout many years of active alcoholism. Families of the addicted understand this factual statement. That skinny fragile thread was a portrait of my puny, human, wearing down, often fickle, inadequate and needy kind of love- *yes*, hanging by a thread, after twenty three years of this agonizing, unremitting alcoholic pain, loss, trauma and drama. The memories of the marvelous compassionate giving man my son could be while sober, faded into the archives of my mind. Praise God that His love for Jared hung not by a human thread but by a three foot thick unbreakable rope-as does His love for you and I. That is the portrait in my own mind of the kind of love God has for us.

So there I was this morning with the following visual in my mind-my son, in extremely dire straights and out of his own mind with severe alcohol poisoning yet once again, was wandering the streets of Boston in this critical condition. He had been severely attacked once in his past while laying in a gutter in New York, passed out in the wee hours of the morning. He was unable to help himself then, and now. Dr. Minor, an expert in the disease of alcoholism who works in the Boston municipal court system had made it clear to me the previous October that "your son is going to die of his alcoholism, you have to start from knowing he is dead, and work backwards from there" he had said. (it came to my mind later that this is exactly how our God works with us in the spiritual realm) This man in the heart of the court system had "seen it all" in horrific detail *over and over again* as far as drunkards dying of their progressive disease. He was very burnt out on parents, especially mothers, who are unable in a sad, tragic, and pitiful way to "let go." He had been intentionally harsh and minced no words with me. It felt merciless because while I knew he spoke truth, it was painful to allow him to press me into deeper knowledge of these terrifying facts. Was Jared going to be found dead in a gutter somewhere? He had a history of drinking himself into gran mal seizures, and had been known to have severely elevated blood pressures caused by the same, inviting permanent brain damage from stroke.

The Lord brought it to my mind that my weapon was prayer on this Florida morning, and I was to contact my Christian sisters at Calvary Chapel in Rockland. Cheryl Cahill, Pastor Randy Cahill's wife had invited me to call the emergency prayer line any time prayer was urgently needed when I had been eating lunch with her and others in the fall of 2019 at their annual Calvary Chapel Women's Retreat. (I had been serving there)

I texted Cheryl, and she instructed me to call Mary at the church who would initiate many sisters to pray for Jared to be located. I called, and Beth answered, a lovely sister in the faith I was familiar with. Mary wasn't there at the moment, but Beth got things going, and she also prayed with me on the phone.

Well Jeff the hotel manager not only ran after Jared that day, he apparently felt inspired to track him back to his apartment, and persuaded him to head back to Yotel Hotel with him. Jeff told me later that he did not want to embarrass Jared by having him apprehended at the building where he resided. He was so kind and empathetic. At some point I am told Jeff engaged Officer Joseph D'Angelo for assistance, a policeman who worked in that precinct of Boston. Because all of this was related to me second hand, some of the finer details aren't clear to me.

What I do know is that I waited for some time, but in a surreal state of Spirit-provided calm, to hear back from someone. I knew I had done my part in soliciting spiritual sisters to pray. My husband had gone ahead and taken our grandchildren to lunch, and I was supposed to join them. Just before I was to depart from the condo, my phone rang again. It was Officer Joseph D'Angelo, and after he ascertained that I was Jared's mother, he said to me something to the effect of "Mam I'm calling to let you know that your son is alright."

Relieved that he was alive, my immediate response to the officer was to cry out *"No! He's NOT!"*Given the history, I was mortified that perhaps a police officer doing a routine "wellness check" might deem Jared, albeit extremely drunk, someone that was not in dire danger for death- or at a minimum, a stroke or life threatening seizure, as he obviously was for self inflicting further liver and brain damage. The liver damage was already well documented.

Officer D'Angelo did not disagree, and he immediately responded "Oh yes, I know that, what I mean is I'm just calling to tell you that he is alive." I was greatly relieved to hear that Joseph's assessment agreed with my own understanding. He started asking me many questions regarding Jared's life and background, and solicited many details regarding the course his alcoholism had taken. He asked me about Jared's estranged wife who had moved down south, and to the best of my understanding, that Jared had continued to support, at least partially. Theirs had been a very toxic and volatile relationship, the marriage having occurred almost immediately after he achieved the milestone of his first year of sobriety in early 2014 after leaving the "Men of Valor in Training" live in church program. Apparently Jared had expressed to the officer that his estranged wife's female medical problems were why he was so inebriated this time. Such amazing denial! (every recovered alcoholic will recognize that excuse as a justification to drink, it sadly doesn't take much for people afflicted with this disease to rationalize their way in just *one* heartbeat, into relapse)

I was astounded, and deeply touched at the personal interest that this wonderful police officer was taking in my family situation! I couldn't believe that there was such another good person (in addition to Jeff at the hotel) on the other end of the phone! In my heart I knew once again that "it is the Lord." He is *sovereign*, we must never doubt it. We must never forget that "all things work together for good for those who love the Lord." (Roman's 8:28) It is He who provided Jeff, the hotel manager. It is He who provided officer Joseph. It is He who inspired Cheryl Cahill the previous year to generously and lovingly tell me I was welcome to call and request prayer on the women's prayer line at any time. Is the veil off of your eyes, reader? Do you *see? Can you see the sovereignty of God in all these things?*

With great sensitivity and understanding, Joseph told me that he was going to take it upon himself to do all the paperwork necessary to attempt to obtain a court order of apprehension from the West Roxbury court, a Section 35, so that Jared might be legally detained and committed (again) in the interest of preserving his life. I was astounded once again that this man was going out on a limb to act in the best interest of assisting a *stranger*. I felt speechless over what God was doing to intervene. It was apparent to me that Joseph had a compassionate and merciful heart. He followed through, and much later that afternoon called me again to say he had obtained the warrant.

In the interim and prior to that late afternoon call, I finally made it over to the Marche Burette where my husband and three grandchildren were finishing their lunch, seated outside. Although overall I did have this surreal sort of inner calm, I also, after I arrived and sat down, started to feel very "split" down the center. I was simultaneously trying to fulfill two of the important roles I have been given in my life-at the same time. I have *always* been a failure at multitasking, and know that I am wired to focus on and attend to just *one thing at a time*. I'm uncertain whether this is a weakness or a strength, but it is how I work. One role at this moment in time was as the mom of an only child who was an alcoholic in a severe crisis playing out, and the other was as a grandmother who yearned to have quality time and make some more memories with these kiddos who would not be visiting with us very long. I didn't want their time to be tainted by my personal crisis. Just as I started to despair over this strange schizophrenic- like internal "tearing" and lose hope that it was possible to carry out my desires to step up to each role in the same moments of my life, my phone sounded. A text came through to my phone.

"Have I not commanded you? Be strong and courageous. Do not be terrified; do not be discouraged, for the Lord your God will be with you wherever you go."

Joshua 1:9 (NIV)

It was from my dear friend from home in Massachusetts, Laura Statts ! We had stayed in touch somewhat while Curt and I wintered in Florida, and she, I was well aware, was praying for me on another matter. I had zero doubt that her intent was to encourage me! However what was also true is that she'd never spontaneously texted me a *scripture* before, and you must be told that piece lest you think this was common between us. She has been blessed with the spiritual gifts of helper and encourager and of providing generous service to others in the church, especially the children, and more. I can not attest to the exact details of what made her choose that text and send it in that moment, but that is no matter. She did it in the power and at the directive of the Holy Spirit within her, I know that much is true. Oh, let's thank God for saints that act on the promptings from within!

You see, not only did I desperately need to hear from God in that very moment as I internally had begun to split, but that verse is the exact same one I had used to encourage my son *often* since he first entered the year long faith based recovery program at Calvary Chapel North Shore (later changed to Great Rock) in 2013. I had written it to him on cards, given him a coffee cup with it inscribed on it, an engraved wall scripture, and had felt prompted by the Spirit myself to mention it to him several times throughout the years. Now I was certain that God was speaking it to *me*, though Laura. God's timing is eternally perfect. The fact that the bible chapter and verse number of 1/9 is Jared's birthday, made it even more personal in my mind, an example of a myriad of ways our God might speak to connect "the dots" with His own. I was reminded not to be terrified or discouraged. I was to rely on God's presence within me, not my flesh, which was presently collapsing under pressure.

As it turned out in the end, it took six days from that Thursday for Jared to be located again, and apprehended and brought into court for a hearing. This type of warrant can't be carried out on a weekend, and Officer Joseph had been off on Friday. On Monday and Tuesday he could not locate Jared and suspected that he was in the hospital, which apparently he was. By the time Jared was discharged from Mass General, picked up by Joseph, and brought to the West Roxbury Court on Wednesday, he was in much better condition(at least on the outside)- and to everyone's surprise the new judge who heard his plea did not commit him to a "treatment" center. That was shocking.

On a side note, and let's remember all of God's side notes are amazing, when a social worker named Courtney called me just prior to that hearing in order to gather more alcoholic history so she could make the case for detainment and commitment, she told me she would call me back in Florida and let me know the outcome (as did officer Joseph). She followed through, and made the call to me about an hour after her pre-hearing call. Courtney was filled with regret, apology, and dismay as she related the report of the judge's decision to me. The judge decided not to forcefully commit him. It seemed to me as if Courtney was blaming herself, and my heart hurt for her as she made it clear to me she felt as if she had failed to accomplish a good thing in my son's behalf. I comforted her, and told her about my God and why I was absolutely fine with the outcome, as I believe God is in control of *all things,* and that Jared's release must be His will.

I had *no doubt that my son had been praying too.* Yet despite God's great mercy and compassion, within a few weeks he was back at Mass General for more detox. This is what my eyes could *see,* and thus I leaned more deeply into the *unseen.*

❀ ❀ ❀

"He has shown you, O mortal, what is good. And what does the Lord require of you? To act justly and to love mercy and to walk humbly with your God."

Micah 6:8 (NIV)

"But thanks be to God, who *put into the heart of Titus* the same earnest care I have for you."

2 Corinthians 8:16
(ESV, emphasis by author)

CHAPTER EIGHTEEN

"Though the fig tree does not bud
and there are no grapes on the vines,
though the olive crop fails
and the fields produce no food,
though there are no sheep in the pen
and no cattle in the stalls
yet I will rejoice in the Lord,
I will be joyful in God my Savior."

Habakkuk 3:17, 18 (NIV)

✠ *IN THE YEAR* 2011, my believing younger sister Diane and I invited my nephew Bill's wife Amy, a fairly new believer at the time, and my deceased sister Jan's daughter Annekje (Bill's sister), a non believer at the time, to the annual Calvary Chapel Women's Retreat. The month for this has always been November. They were both eager to come and spend time with their grandmother and two aunts, but most likely were further motivated by different personal reasons.

Actually, to lay some groundwork for the story so you can appreciate how the Lord was at work even more so, I will digress back to the year 2007, fours years prior to this particular retreat. That is the year that with great sadness and reluctance I stopped attending Calvary Chapel Boston in Rockland, where Pastor Randy Cahill is the senior pastor. I continued with my regular church attendance but did so by going to Calvary Chapel North Shore. I did not feel as if God had left me with any choice in the matter of changing churches, and I was sinfully angry about feeling I must leave the South Shore church and continue at the (much closer) North Shore church. Resentment percolated in my heart when it became obvious at one point that in order to honor my mother, I had to choose to leave the church where my eyes were first opened to God's truth, a church whose pastors and God seeking community I deeply loved in my spirit and my soul.

The previous year in August 2006, my beloved 84 year old dad had taken ill with cardiac trouble while my extended family was vacationing on Cape Cod. He eventually ended up being transferred to Brigham and Women's Cardiac Care unit in Boston where he died from complications caused by a heart attack that occurred just moments before the rescheduled triple bypass surgery, which had already been postponed three times, could be performed. There were some poor medical judgments made by less experienced staff that led to dad's final demise *however* my sister and I understood by faith that God *never* takes anyone home by mistake. His timing is perfect. Thus our faith brought comfort and solace as we were well able to frame the timing of Dad's death as God's ordained will. From mid August until my dad passed mid September, I drove my mother from her home in Lynn to the hospital in Boston daily and spent all day with her there. I took a leave from my work at Brigham and Women's hospital to do this.

While this medical crisis was unfolding within the heart of my family, I had a former commitment to speak at a large medical conference at the Hines Center in Boston, which was scheduled for late January, 2007. I was on their schedule on a Friday to do *two* three hour presentations, six hours of speaking in one day. While I had done a few speaking engagements with several doctors in the pulmonary group I had worked with in former years of my career, I had never previously done anything this large. I would be presenting to huge audiences of professionals. It was an intimidating endeavor. All my prep work had to be done outside of the hours of my nursing position at BWH, since my invitation to speak was not job related.

Thus, the time frame that my beloved dad went into his medical crisis was the same time frame that I had designated to begin spending *all* of my free time working on my two three hour presentations. I had a voluminous amount of preparatory reading and research and organization to do, including preparing two power point programs which I had no former experience doing. My father's cardiac event and my subsequent dedication to supporting my mother through her long sorrowful days led to a delay of about six weeks in beginning my presentation preparatory work. By the time I finally got started at the end of September, after my dad's passing, I knew I was already well behind schedule having lost significant time.

At that time, I was attending Calvary Chapel Boston in Rockland MA, and living in Salem. It was a sizable commute to get to Rockland on Sundays, well over an hour and through Boston, but that is where I was drawn to. The Lord had placed a burning desire on my heart to go and get spiritually fed *there*. Indeed, the Lord grew me through the teaching of God's word. (not through participating in ceremony nor rituals) He had divinely orchestrated in this time of my life the burning need, desire, and freedom to spend extra hours on the road every Sunday, without taking away from anyone else. I was single. My elderly dad and mom had one another, and lived independently. My son was twenty six and on his own. I was free to go to a more distant church and the extra hours spent commuting were of no consequence to me, compared to what I received in return spiritually for my small efforts in making the commute.

With the conference date looming ahead in late January however, as the weeks went by I became increasingly anxious over getting myself properly prepared on time. My job exhausted me during the week, and all I had were Saturday and Sundays to do this extensive work. Without doubt the Christmas season would also detract from the free time I had left. I began to wonder if I should temporarily switch over to a closer church, but just until my conference presentations were over, in order to buy more time on Sundays to prepare my long talks.

One night in November, while driving home from Boston and listening to Christian radio, I heard Pastor Mat Nadworny speaking and did not realize until the end of the program that this was the young pastor that I had heard about through my sister. He had started a Calvary Chapel on the North Shore. He sounded solid, was clearly one hundred percent Biblically based, and he had zeal. I felt as if the Lord was assuring me that it was alright to make the temporary shift over to a closer church to give myself the chance to transform my commuting to church hours, into work hours. Thus near the end of the year, I made the switch to the near church, while planning to return to the Rockland church on the first week of February 2007, after the conference. I was delighted on my first week of attendance that I could see that the new young driven pastor loved the Lord and was indeed zealous for the faith. The congregation was quite tiny, and at that time his small flock met at the Holiday Inn in Peabody on Route One. It was not unusual for the Lord to raise up pastors and grow Calvary Chapel non denominational churches in this way. Some of their stories are written about in a book titled "Harvest" by Pastor Chuck Smith, a true man of God. It contains wondrous testimonies of actual ways our God chooses the apparently weak and foolish things of the world (from a haughty, boastful, elitist world view) to display His power. (1 Corinthians 1:27-28)

January came. I continued with my temporary church- switch plan. Simultaneously, this particular January 2007 was the first my mother was experiencing the fresh and raw agony of widowhood after a blessed loving marriage of fifty eight years. She was deeply grieving, reeling from the loss, and was comforted by the love of her two remaining daughters. (my sister Jan having died eleven years before) Mom had not attended any church since sometime in the late nineteen sixties or very early seventies, almost forty years, as I mentioned in an earlier chapter. She herself did not ascribe to all of what the Catholic church taught, and she felt she had aptly completely her duty of motherhood by introducing her three daughters "to some sort of religion" during their upbringing. Catholicism was the one she was familiar with, and for that reason she chose that "religion". She often asked me "how do you like the new church?" and I would reply in the affirmative that I liked it very much. Majorly motivated by her loneliness, and also on a quest to spend more time with *me* because she had more time on her hands now, she asked me if I would take her to this new church. Thus I took her with me two or three times in January 2007, and she really enjoyed going. Pastor Mat was down to earth, genuine and humble. He preached with fervor for the inerrant truth of the Bible and confessed his own sin and failings with ease to the congregation. I do not believe that my mother was convicted of the truth of the Gospel at the time.

When the time came for me to return to my beloved Rockland Church, mom wanted to remain going to the North Shore Calvary Chapel Church. My heart was still ingrained with the Rockland Church, and the Lord had put on my heart an affinity to my sisters in Christ there, although because I lived so far, many of them didn't know me very well; some not at all, since my work hours and distance from the church was a solid barrier to my participating in deeper fellowship and activities during the week. My mother had fallen in love with Pastor Mat's preaching and *also* with spending most of the day Sunday with me, because we would would go to lunch together after church, and I'd help her do any errands. I realized with a great wrenching of my heart that I must continue to take her there, to Calvary Chapel North Shore, on Sundays. I kept thinking of the commandment to "honor your mother and father" and felt so sad that doing so in this case was going to render what I perceived as a tremendous loss to me. I would have to leave the spiritual leaders and teachers and congregation from Rockland Calvary Chapel completely behind, and I'd had such limited access to them as it was. Perhaps I felt a miniscule taste of the brand of pain Paul had experienced when he was away from or had to depart from the church colonies he had worked fervently to establish while doing his preordained work for Jesus in the first century. (Ephesians 2:10)

Spiritual connection bonds very deeply in the heart, at a depth we can not measure, because it is woven by the Holy Spirit. I know now that God often asks us to do things that will require a form of obedience that seems to greatly *cost* us something. That cost is to our natural hearts and minds, because we think we want one thing, we have planned it on our own, we believe that we have a right to choose it, yet God, through circumstances, tells us to go a different way. That costs us the thing we had been convinced we desired, thought we needed, and had planned. Fortunately, God's mind immeasurably surpasses our own puny ones, and works always to accomplish *His* ultimate plan.

Surrendering to God's will, by letting go of *our* will that rises from our mind ruled by our sin nature is what is meant when we learn through scripture that we are supposed to "die to self" and "pick up our crosses" and follow. We are often blind as to what our next step should be if we are to comply with obedience, but we must be confident that He will orchestrate it through the circumstances that come our way. We *must* be spiritually attentive and in tune with walking by the Spirit. All other roads lead to spiritual death at worst, or at least, missing out on the life we may have lived for God's Kingdom while here-including giving up the fruit God may have brought out of it. His path is always, always superior than the one we lay out for ourselves and the only one from which we can be instruments of God's will being accomplished in and through us, while here. So sisters, allow the gentle yoke and follow with trust and great expectation.

God rewards our obedience and brings us comfort and peace in return for our perceived loss. He sometimes may even later reveal to us retrospectively a bit of what He was doing for the Kingdom. That begets great indwelling joy and spiritual fulfillment. The stronger God has grown your faith, the more confident your expectation of excellent fruit from any set of circumstances will be-and the more you will notice His spiritual "crumbs" on the ground as to the next step He wants you to take, as in the child's fairy tale. Yet remember, His will unfolding does not depend on *your* confidence or lack thereof. Just go. Do what He says. He will teach you *how to know, how to see in the dark where to put your foot down next. If you place it wrongly, your Father will correct you, so do not fear. Move or stay still according to what He has said, always begging Him to purify your heart and refresh you in His Spirit along the way. Do not forget to renew your mind always, as our brother Paul conveyed.*

Our mission is to please an Audience of One. One.

After several years of hearing God's word every Sunday from Pastor Mat, my mother Evelyn was saved. She was born again, yes, a second time, meaning that she was now born into a guarantee of eternal spiritual life during which the spirit of the Lord would spiritually dwell in her inner being while here, imparting life. (John 3) She was no longer a technically "dead woman walking." We are speaking of the spiritual realm when we say this, and of a Kingdom which is not of this world. The Lord had made her a citizen, as was his plan since before the beginning of time. (Ephesians 1:4) The hearing and power of the word had convicted her. I had the privilege and joy of witnessing her walk up to the front of the church in temporal time, and confess her newly born faith to Pastor Mat.

So now it was a couple of years later, 2011 where I started this story. My mother, Diane, Amy (my nephew's wife) and myself were all professed Christ followers. My niece Annekje (whose mom had died years ago) was not, and we were all going to the Calvary Chapel's Women's Retreat together. This was held at the Marriott Hotel in Quincy Massachusetts that year.

Annekje was in her mid thirties at that time and similar to myself, had been leading a Godless life based on ascribing to world values, for a long time. She had experienced much life pain including severe ongoing marital troubles, a highly volatile relationship with her husband, and she bore the emotional wounds and scars of growing up with an alcoholic father who'd been unfaithful to her mother. In his own weakness, he had abandoned my sister Jan in her hour of greatest need. He had his own demons, yes, as we all do- and I do not judge him, because it is not my place. Annekje's mother, Jan, had died later in the same year that Annekje first married, at the young age of twenty. She suffered with the anguish and heartache of losing her wonderful devoted mother at such a young age, when most of us still need them so. She had intermittently spoken about her own struggles with trying not to lean often on the medicinal effects of alcohol, and at times had been caught up in using recreational drugs. She was raising one daughter.

The conference opened with the first teaching on Friday night. All of us sat in a middle row together. I recall that my niece Annekje sat on my right that evening. She pretty much admitted to us all that she was joining us "just to be with us", to spend family time with us. I believe it was our dearest Amy who had invited her along, and we were happy to have her. You see, Annekje had experienced a truly grotesque break of many bones in her right foot a few weeks prior, while carrying laundry down her cellar stairs, and was unable to do much at all! She had eight pins holding her foot bones together! She could only ambulate with crutches. I have no doubt her boredom from being disabled was a motivator to lead her to consent to coming to this conference with us. She was looking for ways to pass the time.

I don't recall if I'd checked on what the Biblical subject matter of this conference was beforehand, in former years it had always been communicated to the women prior to the conference. I don't think I had paid attention to whatever e-mails or information I had been privy to, for in those days I was "very busy." I just knew and trusted however that Calvary Chapel Women's Retreats were always very spiritually rich and edifying, that the Holy Spirit's movement was palpable, that the teachers presenting were always true daughters of the Lord, and I yearned to attend them every year! God has never allowed my thirst for renewal and growth and moving closer to Him to be quenched since making me His. By the end of that first evening it had been made clear to all attending that the scripture verses being taught on at this retreat were Habakkuk 3:17-19.

Suddenly, the Holy Spirit brought it to my mind that my deceased sister Jan's favorite book, second to the Bible itself, was "Hind's Feet in High Places" by Hannah Hurnard. The message in this book is based on the scriptures Habakkuk 3:17-19. This powerful and timeless spiritual allegory dramatizes the victory God accomplishes in His children as He leads them to new heights through many trials and obstacles, that often seem insurmountable. Only *now* did it begin to become clear that God had gotten Annekje here to her first Christian Retreat, and was going to use the coincidences around her beloved mother's favorite Christian book (second to the Bible!) to speak to and minister to *her*. Oh, how my dying sister Jan had prayed for her children! (me too, I was still a heathen when she died)

This story gets even better. As we were all being dismissed from the first session around nine thirty p.m. that Friday evening, I turned to my niece Annekje and said "This is just amazing, your mom's favorite Christian book is rooted in the teaching of these very lines of scripture they are teaching on this weekend!" The "coincidence" was astonishing and could not be ignored. Yet, it became evident very soon to us that God had divinely engineered even more. Annekje said to me "Auntie Mel, just before I left home to come here and meet you all, at the last minute I grabbed a book off of the shelf that has something to do with Christianity, a book that belonged to my mother. I'm not sure what it is. I have to go and check-it's in my suitcase."

Just a brief time later she was pounding on the door of my mom and my and Diane's hotel room, overcome with amazement and gleefully waving "Hind's Feet In High Places" in the air. Not even knowing what it was, she had been prompted by "something" to run and take "a Christian book" that had belonged to her mother off of the shelf before she left home, and bring it along. Do you see how the Holy Spirit is working with God's children even before they have turned over their hearts to Him? He often has things happen to us *before*, so that we can see His hand in it *after*. I can personally testify that this is one of the immeasurable amount of ways He builds the faith of His kids.

The bulk of the teachings occurred the next day on Saturday, and dear Sandy MacIntosh, a mature saint and faithful disciple of Kay Smith, Pastor Chuck Smith's wife, was doing the teaching this year. A piece of her teaching involved a personal testimony that was about a time in her earlier life, decades ago, when she had become extremely discouraged and disheartened by the disability that she experienced after a *severe breaking of multiple bones occurred in her right foot*. It required surgery and the placement of multiple pins, *just like Annekje now,* and a long duration of immobility in order to recover. In fact, on doctor's orders she had to be in a hospital bed for some weeks in the middle of her living room. She had five young children at that time.

Sandy's main point in sharing this testimony with us women was to encourage us in the belief that *nothing will happen to one of the Lord's daughters that He has not ordained for their good.* NOTHING. I recall that she described in detail how frustrated she was with the Lord that this had happened to her, and she could not understand one bit His allowing her to be in a position where she could not care for her children. "Why Lord?" she kept crying out. It was a great spiritual crisis for her, and she agonized in her confusion as to what the Lord was up to in her life. How could she honor the Lord by being a good Christian mother if she had to remain in a hospital bed in the middle of her home- only getting up with crutches to use the bathroom- for many weeks? How could *she do do do* a multitude of tasks that she considered absolutely essential to everyone's well being? But God... *but* God...*but* God...showed her...and He made His answer clear.

Well, Sandy went on to tell us all that *that* period of weeks during which the Lord *forced her to be still* ended up being one of the very most treasured periods of her mothering years that she could *ever* recall! Her young ones would climb into the hospital bed with her located centrally in the house, snuggle, and they would talk and talk, and they had *one hundred percent* of her attention. She told us that she enjoyed her children as she never ever had before- while she was busy *doing*. These disabled weeks evolved into something priceless, an amazing *gift* from the Lord to *her*. It was an incredible time of rest, healing, spiritual growth, and most of all- the opportunity to cultivate deeper relationships, trust and love with the children God gave to her.

It had been delivered in a package that had "disaster" written all over it.

Therefore dear readers, do not lose heart. This will happen to you, too.

As for Annekje, she heard the Lord loud and clear because it is He who had prepared the ground of her heart for the seeds. I watched her countenance as she clearly rejoiced inwardly and outwardly too, as she walked out of the conference room with the rest of us that Saturday afternoon. In fact, that very afternoon she chose to be baptized in the pool by Pastor Randy, alongside my eighty two year old mother Evelyn, her grandmother, who had been planning to get baptized for some time now. Evelyn would depart to be in heaven, in only three more years.

❋ ❋ ❋

"Be still, and know that I am God; I will be exalted among the nations, I will be exalted in the earth."

Psalm 46:10 (NIV)

"Since then, you have been raised with Christ, set your hearts on things above, where Christ is seated at the right hand of God. Set your mind on things above, not on earthly things. For you died, and your life is now hidden with Christ in God."

Colossians 3:1-3 (NIV)

"I have testimony weightier than that of John. For the very works that the Father has given to me to finish, and which I am doing, testify that the Father has sent me."

John 5:36 (NIV)

CHAPTER NINETEEN

"For I know the plans I have for you," declares the Lord,
"plans to prosper you and not to harm you, plans to give
you hope and a future."

Jeremiah 29:11 (NIV)

✝ *THIS WILL BE A SHORT CHAPTER* but please dear reader, do not
miss it's significance. The endless myriad of ways God speaks
to His children and gives them assurance, comfort, guidance, hope,
rescue from themselves and establishes deeper faith, are not
calculable by man. We are not able to understand the mysterious
ways of our Lord, which are beyond *all* of our minds, and thus we
must be diligent to not try and put it all in a tidy box. We must have
confidence *only* in the truths of God's word, and all personal
revelation provided to us that aligns itself with the absolute truth
found the Word- recognized by us via the Spirit within. It's by the
Holy Spirit in us we are made able to discern the spiritual things.
He *makes* us able to discern His activities in our lives at times as it
will prosper us, or spiritually prosper someone else, or advance any
of His other purposes. Perhaps He gave me this little story and the
next one in the next chapter specifically to share with *you* dear one,
if you find this book came into your hands.

As I mentioned in a former chapter, one of my favorite Bible
verses has always been Jeremiah 29:11. Surely this verse speaks to
God's children in a powerful way. Thus there was a New Year's day,

maybe 2014 or 2015, when the morning devotional I was reading at the time was written based on the essence of the meaning of this encouraging scripture verse. That is probably not uncommon- for the Holy Spirit to bring this verse to the mind of God's children at the time of the new calendar year. Having read Jon Courson's book "A Future and a Hope" during my years of approaching and preceding being saved, searching, but still remaining deeply enmeshed by and dancing unaware with the power of sin over me- the message in the devotional, and especially of this verse, was personally very dear to me.

I was delighted to read it in my devotional ("Jesus Calling" by Sarah Young) early that New Year's morning, and thanked God for inspiring me so by the timing. It exhorted me, and lifted my heart spiritually. I thought to myself that later I would post Jeremiah 29:11 on my Facebook page. As I had renewed my mind that morning, my feet felt like the feet of a deer, able to traverse any mountain.

Later that very same day, in the afternoon, my husband Curt and I went to the Marshall's Department store in Florida (where we had arrived earlier than usual for our "snowbirding" months that year). I forget what item exactly he wanted to pick up, but my own desire was to buy myself a nice coffee mug. I have been quite fussy about the cup I drink my morning coffee out of for a long time. I like it to have a certain "feel" and weight in my hand, and my finicky standard on this is often not satisfied by the regular cups in whatever unit we have rented for the season.

Curt found what he wanted, and we approached the cashiers to pay for it. It was then that I remembered my own mission to purchase a special cup just for me, which had momentarily escaped my often feeble mind. I moved my eyes to where they might be, because this store chain often displays many such items at the front near the registers. Immediately I spotted one lone white cup on a shelf near the cashier, that from a distance looked "right" according to my whims. It appeared solid and with some weight to it.

I went and picked it up and it *was* nice and "thick" and large enough, and the grip was perfect in my hand. It was white. All those facts shrunk in significance however, when I read what was boldly written in black on it, in thick lettering. It was Jeremiah 29:11. In Marshall's. Alone on a shelf-spotted immediately, my eyes landing on it almost instantly after I consciously remembered to check to see if the store had one that met my specifications.

I did make a posting on Facebook that day regarding this, but now with a picture of my cup along with a brief testimony as to how it was a clear gift from the Lord. But do you see that the gift was not actually the cup itself but the *awareness* given to me of *evidence of love* from my Father? God my Father had continued once again to provide to me, His daughter, in an obvious and personal way, testimony of His caring and devotion. The incident was witness to His faithfulness that manifests in *all things, large and small.* There is no means which can be deemed too trivial for Him to use to reveal and affirm His love for us. After all, he has counted the hairs on your head, beloved believer and future believer. You belong to Him.

While writing this chapter the Lord brought to my mind that He gives to every one of us a cup to drink from, while here in our bodies in this present life. It contains the deliciously sweet and the dreadfully bitter, seasonings of pain and agony and also savory splendid richness. He has prepared our cups long ago, his Divine creativity in this activity unfolding with the ultimate love for us and devotion to us, His wayward kids. While drinking from them as we are praying for *His* power and *His* grace to keep us from falling into pits of complaint, self pity, hopelessness and despair, *it is He who will illuminate the way to he or she who asks.* Can we do it willingly? Drink what is in our cup with trust? Can we view every single event and detail in our

Christian walks as occurring for our ultimate spiritual *good?* He is faithful, beloved reader. He is faithful.

> "Then said Jesus unto Peter, "Put up thy sword into the sheath! The cup which my Father has given me, shall I *not drink it?"*

John 18:11
(KJV, emphasis by author)

> "...his compassions never fail. They are new every morning; great is your faithfulness."

Lamentations 3:22-23 (NIV)

CHAPTER TWENTY

✚ *THERE WAS A LITTLE GIRL WHO WAS ABOUT 10 YEARS OLD*, and at her elementary school back in the early 1960's, every year, a Christmas pageant was performed in the gymnasium. There were bleaches on one side of the gymnasium, and during the pageant this is where the robed children's chorus would line up and sing. There was a stage at the front, and on the pageant night all of the parents and grandparents would come to watch and hear the children sing. All the children in her school, Shoemaker School in Lynn, Massachusetts, had a part. Upon the stage there was a live manger scene comprised of the children from grades four through six, that were honored to be selected for these coveted roles. This is the time and place where this little girl learned all of the words to all of the Christmas Carols she knew. Every year she would hear them and practice them with her schoolmates, for about six weeks prior to the pageant. There was "Up On the Rooftop" and "Rudolf the Red Nosed Reindeer", "Here Comes Santa Claus" and a variety of children's traditional songs which were purely fun songs rooted in purely secular traditional celebration of the season. All of those kinds of songs were sung by grades one through three.

The songs that penetrated and drew her heart, however, were the ones that told the story of Christ's birth, rejoiced, and sang of His glory. Songs like "The First Noel" and "Come All Ye Faithful" and "Hark the Herald Angels Sing."Her very favorite song however, was "What Child is This?" and our Lord used it to soften her heart that was a bit hardened and closed off to Him, as a result of her own experiences at her Sunday School, and the love that seemed to have been absent there. This child had never prayed to God personally before. She had, under instruction by the authorities at her Sunday School, repeated in a rote and mechanical fashion, a fashion absent of her heart and faith, the words to a handful of rote prayers she had memorized upon command. The combination of the lyrics and the mesmerizing tune of this particular song touched something waiting deep inside of her to awaken.

What Child is This

What child is this
Who laid to rest
On Mary's lap is sleeping?
Whom Angels greet with anthems sweet,
While shepherds watch are keeping?

Chorus

This, This is Christ the King
Whom shepherds guard and Angels sing!
Haste, haste to bring Him laud,
The Babe, the Son of Mary.

So bring Him incense, gold and myrrh,
Come peasant, King to own him.
The King of Kings salvation brings,
Let loving hearts enthrone Him. (chorus)

Oh raise, raise a song on high,
His mother sings her lullaby.
Joy, oh joy for Christ is born,
The Babe, the Son of Mary!

One year, and this writer fails to recall for certain if it was the fifth or the sixth grade pageant, as the teachers were putting together and directing the Christmas program, they announced that they wanted to select three girls from the fifth or sixth grade to go up onto the stage and sing "What Child is This?" Thus they took some time during one afternoon rehearsal to invite any female child who was interested in being a part of this vocal trio, to "try out for the part." This little girl had an overwhelming desire to be chosen to sing this song. It came from a place of something that was *right* within her, as opposed to wrong. It came from something that was pure, because this desire was *placed into her, not of her.*

You see, her yearning to sing the song publicly was not a function of wanting to receive attention, of wanting to be seen by many, or of seeking exaltation or praise for herself. Not that she was beyond those temptations in any way! In fact, many years later she would struggle enormously with the sin of pride. This *Hope* of being chosen was very different from those carnal desires that she was not exempt from, having been born with a sin nature. She could not really put this difference into words, but she was aware.

She was generally quite shy at school, but somehow was graced with the courage to walk up onto that stage and sing in front of all the other children to try out for the part on that appointed afternoon. Her voice was average, and although she would have liked to think otherwise, she knew she did not compare to her friend Debbie or several other girls in vocal ability. Shaking in her shoes, she tried out anyway. *Then she went home and started talking to God and prayed very hard, in her own words,* that she would be one of the three girls selected, and receive the joy of singing the beautiful melody with the beautiful wondering words contemplating the identity of Jesus on the special night. It was the first genuine prayer she had ever prayed. It was the first time she ever had cried out earnestly for the power of the Father to help her.

God heard this young child's prayer, as He surely hears them all with a tender ear. He granted her petition, and on the following day the ten year old girl was astounded when the teachers announced that her name was on the list of the three chosen! The incredible thing, the astounding thing to this child was that she knew, *she knew,* for the very first time that GOD IS, and the writer looks back and sees that He was speaking to her and proclaiming to her, even way back then- I AM.

For about five or six months following the Christmas pageant, this young girl felt a powerful presence with her at all times, and was acutely aware of it. She knew it was God, and that He had made himself known to her. She rejoiced in her heart, and told no one. Of course, it was the Holy Spirit with her. This sixty seven year old writer remembers the palpable power of this, and still can call to mind the inner wonder of the child and how miraculous it all felt during that period of months.

Eventually, as childhood progressed *she forgot* all about the Presence that had surrounded her and had given her such surprising delightful joy, and a sense of everlasting security and divine power. The great I AM however *never forgot her*, even though many years filled with and dominated by much sin lay ahead.

Dear one, He will never forget you either. He will provide you with whatever it takes for Him to own your heart, if you seek with sincerity for absolute truth. It is good for those who are hesitant to cross the threshhold into new birth to cry out with questions and wrestle before Him with your doubts, and beg for Him to reveal Who He is to you! Do not be dismayed or put off by temporary sufferings, setbacks and turmoil! God has taught me and countless others that His loving mercies often arrive in severe and painful packages in this carnal world, and that Satan's lies often arrive in fetchingly designed bouquets of cunning disguise and appear harmless and fulfilling to the human eye. By the human eye of flesh we are not able to see Him...our Lord, and His truth must be spiritually discerned, because His Kingdom is still unseen at this time in His story. History. Do you know it is all about your Messiah? All.

"This mystery is that through the gospel the Gentiles are heirs together with Israel, members together of one body, and sharers together in the promise in Christ Jesus."

Ephesians 3:6 (NIV)

CHAPTER TWENTY ONE

But what does it say?

"The word is near you; it is in your mouth and in your heart", that is, the word of faith we are proclaiming: That if you confess with your mouth, "Jesus is Lord", and believe in your heart that God raised him from the dead, you will be saved. For it is with your heart that you believe and are justified, and it is with your mouth that you confess and are saved. As the Scripture says, "Anyone who trusts in him will never be put to shame." For there is no difference between Jew and Gentile-the same Lord is Lord of all and richly blesses all who call on him, for "Everyone who calls on the name of the Lord will be saved."

Romans 10:8-13 (NIV)

✝ *BELOVED BELIEVERS, DO NOT EVER DOUBT* that our Jesus, our Lord, who now sits at the right hand of the Father until His return, completes His work in you and through you and shall continue until this age is fulfilled, or until your body dies and you get to go to Him. You get to go to the place He has prepared. Isn't that wonderful? (Phil. 1:21) Everything that happens *to you* is everything that happens *for you*, regardless of what form it comes in. *All* is for the glory of His Eternal Kingdom and has and will be and is being accomplished through the Holy Spirit, *His Spirit* now within you, by whom we have been saved from the spiritual death we were formerly walking in, *through faith*. It is the Spirit who imparts spiritual life. Apart from this there is only death. The Spirit of him who raised Jesus from the dead is living in *you and in me*. Christ is our life.

> "The mind of sinful man is death, but the mind controlled
> by the Spirit is life and peace."

> Romans 8:6 NIV

Yet we are told in Genesis 6:3 that the Lord has said that "my Spirit shall not always strive with man, for he is also flesh..." Why? Why might the Lord have said that in the first book of the Bible and as early in recorded temporal time as Genesis? You see, the chance provided for you and I born spiritually of His grace, and for the remaining unbeliever, to respond to His calling- is and was a measured one, and it does not extend beyond the life of our physical body. Can you see, do you *know* yet that God so loved the world that He sent his only Son to satisfy the commandments and regulations of the holy law, which His children have proven over and over again throughout time we *can not keep? In our fallen state we are unable, we are transgressors, and we need a savior.*

Every. Single. One. All people.

To God's first chosen race, my Jewish sisters and brothers, God's beloved Israel through whom He has *always* planned to bless ALL nations-have you not often wondered or been confused or concerned or puzzled about God's plan for us Gentiles that you so *love*? For religiously observant Jews-have you immersed yourselves so passionately and diligently in studying and pursuing God's holy and perfect law, in the tradition that leads you to do so, that you haven't noticed the veil that is not allowing you to recognize how impossible it is for you *sufficiently* keep it? My Jewish friend, you can no more *wash yourself clean* from the unacceptable- to- God- stain of the inner sin nature by law keeping and ritualistic religious practice than a practicing Catholic can cleanse themselves by acting out human or self assigned penance- or count on the ritual of the beautiful practice of communion, to make oneself presentable to God.

The practice of communion is good, and pleases our God. Every time humans obey a God-directive- whether it was, for one example-in the past, rejoicing during the Feast Of Tabernacles as Jews obediently memorialized the journey from Egypt to the promised land (and still do), or, in the present-sharing a Passover Seder, or God's people now remembering His Son in this age in the way He asked them to, God is pleased with His children.

Communion represents obedience to Christ our Savior's instructive to *remember Him. He has told us that He and the Father are One. "Whoever has seen me has seen the Father." (John 14:9 ESV)* Our Father, throughout the ages, has *continuously* asked that we all remember Him-before, during, and after the coming of our Messiah! In itself, communion practice *reflects* the faith and heart of obedience in God's child. It does not serve to save anyone! No action does-*only belief.* We are to constantly remember what Christ has done for us- that *love came down to do for us what we could not do for ourselves.* Obedience *follows* belief. We can not get to salvation *by the law.*

Genuine Gentile and Jewish (Messianic) Christian practice of faith is *evidence* of what the Lord has done in one of His own. The law for all of us is the same- in that it is *good, holy, from God,* and the one who yearns to keep it for God's sake is treasured. Yet, we must not regard our own ability to keep it as ever being *adequate* to reunite us to God, as a means to regeneration, *which is new life.*

We. Can. Not. Get. There. On. Our. Own.
JESUS.

Refraining from stealing, killing, bearing false witness, lustful activities, dishonoring our parents or making idols of that other than our Holy God all represent forms of obedience to law which are human choices most pleasing to God. He loves it when we choose to obey His commandments! Yet I say again, keeping them are not the *way* to salvation, because sooner or later we *will mess up. That's guaranteed.* That's what the Bible teaches. "Give up on yourself."

Its message is completely counter-cultural during our times.

Christ fills the immeasurable gap between our fickle desire and our inability to satisfy the requirements of a Holy God. Leaving all of our sins, past and present, behind us where God says He no longer sees or counts them against us, is a *result of salvation. The power to be freed of their burden comes from the Holy Spirit within.* Christ paid for our redemption *in full.* FULLY PAID. Do you want it? He speaks to *all,* Jew and Gentile, in the entirety of the scriptures.

How much sin is acceptable to a Holy God? Our perfect God requires perfection if we are to be redeemed by law. We all fail. We can not do it. We are *all* a stiff necked people. Ask God to reveal to you where in your life that is true within *you.* Once you find the fatal flaw(s) in yourself, ask God where then, may you find hope?

Via the nation of Israel, beginning with our human father of faith, Abraham, God has constructed *one way* for *all of us* to become restored to Him. He provided an alternative sacrifice for Abraham in reward to his obedience born of deep faith, trust and dependence, when he was willing to kill a member of his *family,* Isaac, rather than disregard his Lord's instruction. There *"just happened" to be a ram in the thicket.*

Is there one for you? For me?

The answer is *yes,* beloved, He has given us the same, an alternative sacrifice, rather than leave us as *not part of His family.*

We too, like Isaac, were all on our way to literal death, due to the fall. Our merciful God has provided us with an alternative to permanent spiritual death. It is belief in Jesus- faith and trust in His redeeming work, which was finished at the appointed time when He completed carrying out the will of His Father. He submitted to the Father- to allowing His own flesh be *crucified*. When you believe, your flesh is crucified in God's eyes, too. If you believe this you can choose it daily, moment by moment, and have the deeper abundant life *now*.

Can you even imagine what our Father holds in store for those who come to recognize the Way? Our human minds fail completely on being able to absorb the full magnificence of our loving God's plan to extend His grace to *all* of us sinners. His plan to do so was never to *fix* what we are, for that entity bent consistently towards sin must be *willing to die to itself*. Our flesh is not fixable, it's completely corrupt, and it is in *need* of being crucified along with Christ. It was, on the cross! The plan was *always, since before the foundation of time*, for Him to *become our righteousness by fulfilling the law perfectly in our behalf,* and to bring all His willing kids home.

There have been no God- mistakes in the history of the world. It has continued to unfold according to our God's purposes. Can we not see for ourselves that we may be made ONE in Jesus? Built into a temple of *living stones?* He who believes in Jesus will be mightily saved. He will be an eternal member of God's family, a sibling of and an heir with Christ. It is all of us, all believers, Jew and Gentile, who are God's *true* Israel by God's *promise* to Abraham.

"For not all who are descended from Israel are Israel."

(Romans 9:6 NIV)

"A man is not a Jew if he is only one outwardly, nor is circumcision merely outward and physical. No, a man is a Jew if he is one inwardly; and circumcision is a circumcision of the heart, by the Spirit, not by the written code. Such a man's praise is not from men but from God."

Romans 2:28-29 NIV

All believers, Christ followers, are children of the *promise*, exactly as Isaac was a child beget by a promise of God. By supernatural power our God brought a son for Abraham and Sarah into being through a deadened womb. That womb could no more bring life forth of it's own natural ability than water will flow from a rock minus God's command. Neither can we. But He is the God that makes things that are *not as though they are*. Has God made a way for all human beings, the originally chosen and the after sought and found, to be His very own?

Yes! In God's eyes all believers who receive God's son are the true authentic Jews of His spiritual kingdom. It is not about our ethnic origin. It is *not* a function of our genetic heritage! Sin has been passed along through the generations via the flesh, but life in the Spirit has *not*. We must seek it, and submit to God's desire to haul us into the life boat. Yet our days in the flesh are numbered, and dear one, you do not have unlimited time to respond to His calling *you*. His promises are for every believer, and it is never too late *until* you die. There is no salvation after death.

Whether you have acknowledged it or not, Christ has been reaching out to you in your mind and in your heart, all of your life, by many things, starting with making it possible for you to view and enjoy the breathtaking and marvelous inexplicable beautiful complexity of His creation. He has worked within your conscience. Jesus has done all the work to reconcile every Jew and Gentile to God, through the cross. He is written about in detail, foreshadowed and prophesied consistently for many ages throughout *all* the scriptures of the Old Testament, and the books called Torah (which are the first chapters of the Old Testament). You will find Him there in the inspired words, starting with Moses's writings. Moses wrote:

> "The Lord your God will raise up for you a prophet like me from among your own brothers. You must listen to him"- and also, "The Lord said "I will raise up for them a prophet like you from among their brothers; I will put my words in his mouth, and he will tell them everything I command him."
>
> Deuteronomy 18:15,18 NIV

Ask God, even if you still have lingering doubt, to show you what He wants you to (and *will enable you* to) spiritually discern. Be ready for an answer from Him, because He *will reveal spiritual truth to you when you ask.*

Does that surprise you?

Knock, seek, ask. Beloved one, He desires you to come. Read the Bible, *all of it*. The Old Testament establishes the critical foundation of and the miraculous astounding veracity of the New Testament, and neither covenant can possibly be complete without the other. You will see that God did not send Jesus to change inherently bad people (all of us) into good people. He came to give dead people life. He laid His down for you. Will you receive it? Your flesh was crucified on the cross with Jesus, He satisfied the law for *you*, please believe it. Accept what He offers to you through immeasurable *love*.

There are no good people from a spiritual perspective, there is only Christ, who lovingly imparts to sinning people His own Holy life, when they recognize their own weakness and inability, repent, and invite Him in and then follow. Our Jesus came to give dead people life! *He* is what makes them holy, because all believers are the workmanship of a Holy God. It is Jesus Who has come, and Who will save you from spiritual death. He is the way to life and He desires *you* to hear His voice. Will you listen keenly that you may hear it today? He is coming again. He promised. May the Lord open the eyes of every reader. The flesh profits *nothing, work and try as you might, but there is one Hope.*

❖ ❖ ❖

"For the grace of God has appeared, bringing salvation for all people, training us to renounce ungodliness and worldly passions, and to live self-controlled, upright, and godly lives in the present age, waiting for our blessed hope, the appearing of the glory of our great God and Savior Jesus Christ, who gave himself up for us to redeem from all lawlessness and to purify for himself a people for his own possession who are zealous for good works."

Titus 2:11-14 (ESV)

"But Israel will be saved by the Lord with an everlasting salvation; you will never be put to shame or disgraced, to ages everlasting."

Isaiah 45:17 (NIV)

"And in this way all Israel will be saved, as it is written, "The Deliverer will come from Zion, he will banish ungodliness from Jacob;"

Romans 11:26 (ESV)

❉ ❉ ❉

Have you been made Israel beloved? This is the way God's longing is satisfied. Can you see yet? He has always intended that there be *one Shepherd, one flock.*